RACISM
ON TRIAL

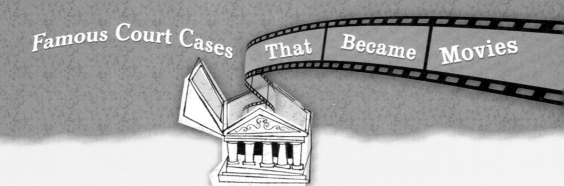

Famous Court Cases That Became Movies

RACISM ON TRIAL

From the
**Medgar Evers
Murder Case**
to
*Ghosts of
Mississippi*

Wim Coleman and Pat Perrin

Enslow Publishers, Inc.
40 Industrial Road
Box 398
Berkeley Heights, NJ 07922
USA

http://www.enslow.com

Library of Congress Cataloging-in-Publication Data

Coleman, Wim.
    Racism on trial : From the Medgar Evers murder case to "Ghosts of Mississippi" /
        Wim Coleman and Pat Perrin.
        p. cm. — (Famous court cases that became movies)
    Includes bibliographical references and index.
    Summary: "Examines the Byron De La Beckwith murder trials, including the
        mistrials and his eventual conviction, key figures in the case, and the inspiration
        for the movie Ghosts of Mississippi"—Provided by publisher.
    ISBN-13: 978-0-7660-3059-6
    ISBN-10: 0-7660-3059-8
        1. Beckwith, Byron de la—Trials, litigation, etc.—Juvenile literature. 2. Evers,
    Medgar Wiley, 1925-1963—Assassination—Juvenile literature. 3. Trials (Murder)—
    Mississippi—Jackson—Juvenile literature. 4. Mississippi—Race relations—Juvenile
    literature. 5. Hate crimes—Mississippi—Jackson—Juvenile literature. 6. Lynching—
    Mississippi—Jackson—Juvenile literature. I. Perrin, Pat. II. Title.
    KF224.B34C65 2009
    345.762'5102523—dc22
                                   2008021483

Printed in the United States of America

9 8 7 6 5 4 3 2 1

To Our Readers:
We have done our best to make sure all Internet addresses in this book were active and appropriate when we went to press. However, the author and the publisher have no control over and assume no liability for the material available on those Internet sites or on other Web sites they may link to. Any comments or suggestions can be sent by e-mail to comments@enslow.com or to the address on the back cover.

♻ Enslow Publishers, Inc., is committed to printing our books on recycled paper. The paper in every book contains 10% to 30% post-consumer waste (PCW). The cover board on the outside of each book contains 100% PCW. Our goal is to do our part to help young people and the environment too!

Illustration Credits: AP/Wide World, pp. 6, 33, 39, 44, 65 (top), 69; Everett Collection, pp. 3, 13, 23, 65 (bottom), 74, 77, 81, 85, 92; Library of Congress, pp. 18, 27, 49, 55, 99.

Cover Illustrations: Courthouse logo—Artville; gavel—Digital Stock; poster for *Ghosts of Mississippi*—Everett Collection.

CONTENTS

Mourners file past the casket of civil rights worker Medgar Evers, assassinated in June 1963 by Byron De La Beckwith.

Chapter 1

The Surprise Witness

If it had not snowed in Chicago on January 28, 1994, Mark Reiley might never have testified against Byron De La Beckwith. As it happened, Reiley became a surprise witness—a surprise to the defense, to the prosecution, and even to himself—in a major murder trial.

In 1963, a man named Medgar Evers had been murdered in Jackson, Mississippi. Although there had been an arrest and two trials, no one was ever convicted of the crime. The unsolved case left a legacy of bitterness, a sense of justice denied. And now, more than thirty years later, Mark Reiley was about to be drawn into a dramatic courtroom confrontation.

Mark Reiley worked for a company that supplied communications equipment to airports. But on that Friday morning, Chicago's O'Hare airport was shut down because of snow. Air traffic controllers were not working, and Reiley did not need to work that day. So the red-haired, thirty-six-year-old junior manager stayed home and watched the news on CNN.

The weather was not the only big story on the news. Reiley also watched reports of the trial about to begin far to the south in Jackson, the capital of Mississippi. The defendant was a seventy-three-year-old man charged with murder. To Reiley's amazement, he recognized the man on trial. He even remembered some of that man's words—hateful, bragging words. As Reiley thought back, he realized that the man had been talking about this very crime.

Mark Reiley picked up his telephone and called District Attorney Ed Peters in Hinds County, Mississippi. Soon after making the call, he found himself on a plane headed south.

The Big Story on TV

The 1994 trial of Byron De La Beckwith for the 1963 murder of Medgar Evers fascinated the American public. The victim had been a well-known civil rights activist and a field officer for the National Association for the Advancement of Colored People (NAACP). But it had taken a long, long time for this trial to come to court.

This was the third time that Beckwith was tried for the murder of Medgar Evers. The first two trials, back in 1964, had been declared mistrials. Now prosecutors were trying to make a new case against Beckwith.

Why Could Byron De La Beckwith Be Tried Three Times for the Same Crime?

Being tried more than once for the same offense—called "double jeopardy"—is illegal. If a defendant is found "not guilty," he or she cannot be retried for the same offense. However, if the jury cannot reach a verdict, the judge can declare a mistrial.

After a mistrial, the case can be tried again without causing double jeopardy, and both of Beckwith's 1964 trials were declared mistrials. Although Beckwith's lawyers objected to the 1994 trial on the basis of double jeopardy, the Mississippi Supreme Court rejected their claim.

Their story has been told in songs, books, and films, including a 1996 movie, *Ghosts of Mississippi.*

It had been hard for anyone to find out what had happened so long ago. A lot of the records from 1964 were missing. Evidence used at those trials had been lost. Most people had doubted that there could even be a third trial. Surely, many believed, a third trial would also result in a mistrial.

Bobby DeLaughter's Questions

The Hinds County, Mississippi, assistant district attorney (DA) had been investigating this case for five years.

Assistant DA Bobby DeLaughter was convinced that Byron De La Beckwith committed the crime. He could not understand how the man had gotten away with murder.

Prosecuting Beckwith would become difficult and costly for DeLaughter. The young lawyer would find important evidence, but he would also make at least one serious mistake. Some people would criticize DeLaughter for moving too fast; others would complain that he was moving too slowly. The young lawyer would face family problems and physical threats.

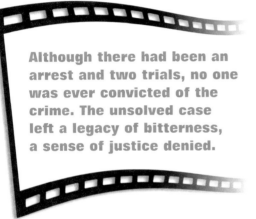

Although there had been an arrest and two trials, no one was ever convicted of the crime. The unsolved case left a legacy of bitterness, a sense of justice denied.

Clearly, the easiest thing to do would have been to leave the old case alone. But DeLaughter had too many unanswered questions. He said, "I felt like not only myself but also Mississippi was being put to the test. . . . Basically, for me it was put up or shut up time for everything I believed in legally and morally."[1]

The "Instruction" of Mark Reiley

When Mark Reiley said that he recognized Byron De La Beckwith, DeLaughter had his story checked out. Yes, the attorney discovered, Reiley could have known Beckwith. The two men had been in the same place at the same time. There had been plenty of opportunity for the conversations that Reiley said he remembered.

Why Could Byron De La Beckwith Be Tried Thirty Years After the Crime Took Place?

A "statute of limitations" sets time limits on the prosecution of many crimes, but there is no statute of limitations for murder. So no time limits prevented Beckwith from being tried thirty years after the murder took place.

The Sixth Amendment of the U.S. Constitution grants the accused the right to a "speedy trial" once charges have been brought. Beckwith's lawyers claimed a 1994 trial would be a violation of the defendant's right to a speedy trial. However, the Mississippi Supreme Court made no decision on the speedy-trial issue, and the case moved ahead.

Byron De La Beckwith had spent part of the 1970s at Angola Penitentiary in Baton Rouge, Louisiana. Acting on a tip from the Federal Bureau of Investigation (FBI), New Orleans police had stopped Beckwith on the highway to New Orleans. When they searched his car, the police officers discovered a bomb and other weapons. Beckwith also had a map, marked to show the home of an important Jewish leader—the man who headed the New Orleans chapter of the Anti-Defamation League (an organization that fights discrimination against Jews). Beckwith served a three-year sentence for possession of a bomb.

In 1979, young Mark Reiley was working as a guard in the prison ward of the Earl K. Long Hospital in Baton Rouge, Louisiana. Prison inmate Beckwith became ill and was sent to the hospital's prison ward. Beckwith took an instant liking to the young guard of Scots-Irish background.

"Hey, Young Blood," Beckwith called when Reiley first walked into the room.[2]

Over the next several weeks, the two men spent eight to ten hours a day together, talking and studying the Bible. Beckwith acted like a father figure to the young guard. At first, Reiley had been happy for the company and discussions with the older man. But eventually Beckwith's words began to trouble Reiley.

Over the years, Reiley had mentioned his disturbing conversations with a prisoner to a few people. But finally, he had forgotten all about Beckwith. When he saw the news about the trial, Reiley had realized for the first time exactly what Beckwith had been bragging about.

Mark Reiley's Memories

During their Bible studies, Reiley had learned what the scriptures meant according to Byron De La Beckwith. The prisoner had insisted the Bible said that white people were God's chosen people.

According to Beckwith, African Americans were meant to be dominated by whites. Since black people were just beasts of the field, he said, they could be killed without any feelings of guilt. At first, Reiley paid little attention to this dark side of Beckwith's "religious beliefs."

Byron De La Beckwith is led away to jail by FBI agents after his 1963 arrest for the murder of Medgar Evers. It would be more than thirty years before Beckwith was brought to justice.

One day when Beckwith pushed a call button to summon a nurse, an African-American nurse's aide came to help him. Beckwith demanded that a white person come instead. The patient and the nurse's aide got into an argument, yelling at each other.

Finally, Beckwith screamed, "If I could get rid of an uppity nigger like nigger Evers, I would have no problem with a no-account nigger like you."[3]

Reiley had no idea who Medgar Evers was. But after that outburst, he began to listen more carefully to what Beckwith was saying. The older man tried to draw Reiley into his organization. The group's purpose was to prove the superiority of whites. They taught that "blacks, if necessary, needed to be eliminated."[4]

When Reiley began to question Beckwith's views, the prisoner argued with him. Beckwith bragged about having escaped conviction for a much bigger crime. He claimed that if he was not such an important man, "he would be serving time in jail in Mississippi for getting rid of that nigger Medgar Evers."[5]

Changes in the South

A lot had changed since the first two trials of Byron De La Beckwith for the murder of Medgar Evers. In 1964, the juries had been all white men, and they had deadlocked at about half and half. By 1994, both men and women were serving on racially diverse juries.

During the earlier trials, white community sympathy had been with Beckwith. At that time, a witness testifying against a white person in a racially charged trial might be attacked, even murdered. Now, many white citizens were eager to move beyond the racial conflicts

Missing from the Movie

Even though District Attorney Ed Peters called Mark Reiley his "cleanup hitter," that character was left out of the movie *Ghosts of Mississippi*. By eliminating the last-minute excitement of a new witness, the movie focused attention on Bobby DeLaughter's intense final speech as the main reason for the verdict.

of the past, and witnesses were less fearful of retaliation for testifying.

As David Sansing, professor emeritus of history at the University of Mississippi, told *The New York Times* in 1999:

> In the South, we now have a black constituency that has political clout and a white constituency that is not against these hate-mongers being brought to justice. . . . And the black constituency, emboldened by newfound political power, is saying, "Justice delayed is justice denied, so let's quit denying this justice." Surprisingly, they are being met with sympathy from district attorneys.[6]

By 1994, Hinds County, Mississippi, assistant DA Bobby DeLaughter was intent on seeing the murderer of Medgar Evers finally brought to justice. Some citizens had decided over time that they should tell what they knew about Byron De La Beckwith. Others, like Reiley, had not even heard about the earlier trials but were ready to testify in this one.

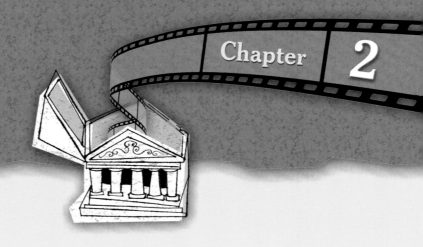

Chapter 2

Assassination

It was June 12, 1963. In Jackson, Mississippi, a man holding a high-powered .30-06 caliber Enfield rifle with a telescopic sight waited behind a thicket of bushes and honeysuckle vines. He was a gun-lover, hunter, and marksman who had spent many hours target shooting.

From where he was hidden, the gunman had a clear view of a private home about two hundred feet away. He kept his attention on the driveway in front of the house. Sooner or later, the man he intended to kill would return home.

The man who lived in that house arrived a little after midnight. He parked his car in his driveway, got out, and headed for his front door. A shot rang out.

▮▯▮▯▮▯▮▯▮▯▮▯▮▯▮▯▮▯▮▯▮▯▮▯▮▯▮▯▮▯▮▯▮▯▮

A bullet struck the victim in the back, passed completely through his body, and smashed the living-room window. The deadly slug passed through a wall on the other side of the living room, sped across the kitchen, ricocheted off the refrigerator, smashed a glass coffeepot, and finally came to rest on a countertop.

Inside that house, the victim's family knew what the sound must mean. The children dove for the floor, as they had been trained to do. Their mother rushed to the front door and turned on the light. Then they all ran outside to see what had happened.

Myrlie Evers found her husband lying face down in the driveway. A trail of blood showed where he had dragged himself nearly forty feet toward his home after being shot. Scattered around him were the sweatshirts he had been carrying. They bore the slogan "Jim Crow Must Go."

Screaming, Myrlie and the children ran to the fallen man. The children cried over and over, "Daddy, Daddy, please get up."[1] But Medgar Evers could barely move.

Neighbors also knew what the sound of a gun might mean. One neighbor ran into his yard, fired a shot into the air, and shouted, "There's a killer in the neighborhood!"[2] Neighbors and policeman soon arrived at the scene of the shooting. They put the bleeding man onto a mattress, lifted him into a station wagon, and rushed him to the nearest hospital.

At the University Hospital, the victim faced a slight delay. Since the facility was open to whites only, the black man was at first refused admission. But hospital administrators quickly realized that the victim was a

What Did "Jim Crow Must Go" Mean?

State and local laws that governed segregation in the American South from 1876 to 1965 were widely referred to as Jim Crow laws. The name is believed to have originated about 1830 with a white comedian's song and dance act. Thomas "Daddy" Rice wore blackface makeup (charcoal or burned cork). He performed what was supposed to be the ridiculous song and dance of a crippled black man. The song's chorus ended with the words "Jump Jim Crow." The Jim Crow character became a standard in minstrel shows (a type of entertainment popular in the nineteenth century involving white comedians, musicians, and dancers wearing blackface makeup). The name was used as a racial slur, and discriminatory laws were called Jim Crow laws.

A nineteenth-century engraving shows the white minstrel-show performer "Daddy" Rice portraying the character Jim Crow, a term later applied as a racial stereotype to discriminatory laws.

well-known person. The hospital admitted him, but Evers died less than an hour later.

The Murdered Man

Medgar Wiley Evers was a native of Mississippi. Born in Decatur on July 2, 1925, he attended segregated public schools. For African-American children, going to school meant long walks, outdated textbooks, and large numbers of students packed into small, poorly equipped classrooms.

Southern black youngsters in those days faced violent racism. At age fourteen, Medgar saw a friend of his father's dragged through the streets behind a wagon. The man, who had been accused of insulting a white woman, was shot and hanged by furious white citizens. Every day on his way to school, young Evers walked past the dead man's bloody clothes that had been left on the ground near the hanging tree.

By the time Medgar Evers was seventeen, the United States was embroiled in World War II. His brother Charles, whom Medgar idolized, had joined the U.S. Army. Medgar left high school and also volunteered for service. He served in Great Britain and in France, fighting in the ferocious Battle of Normandy.

Like everything else in Evers's life, his army battalion was segregated. African-American soldiers served under white officers and were assigned to the dirtiest jobs, such as cleaning latrines. But in Europe, Evers had one completely new experience—white people treated him as an equal.

By the time he returned home from the war, Medgar Evers was ready for a different kind of battle—one for

Was Racial Segregation Legal?

Segregation laws were customary in the South. In 1896, an African American named Homer Plessey had been arrested and convicted in Louisiana for riding in a railway car that was designated for whites only. Plessey challenged his conviction and took his case to the U.S. Supreme Court, but the justices voted in favor of Louisiana. The Supreme Court said that segregation could remain legal as long as the facilities were "separate but equal."

the full rights of citizenship. In the Southern United States, Jim Crow laws were in effect. He intended to challenge those laws.

Jim Crow laws made it illegal for African Americans to drink from water fountains or use public restrooms marked for white use. Black people could not enter public parks and other recreational areas or eat in public restaurants. And the facilities open to them, including schools, were far from equal to the facilities used by whites.

In addition to those segregation laws, many illegal actions prevented African Americans from voting. Medgar Evers's wife, Myrlie, later commented that even registering to vote could bring retaliation.

Their names would be published in the newspaper with their addresses and phone numbers, and they would be harassed by phone calls, people driving by, throwing rocks, eggs, firebombs. . . . Or the banks would call in mortgages with no notice. People got fired from their jobs immediately. Or lassoed as they were walking home, dragged into a car [and then beaten]. All this because they wanted to vote.[3]

Of course, if African Americans could not vote, they could do nothing to change those Jim Crow laws. In the summer of 1946, Medgar Evers, his brother Charles, and several other black veterans registered to vote at the Decatur city hall. On election day, a crowd of angry white citizens gathered at the courthouse. Armed white men blocked their entrance into the clerk's office and kept them away from the polls.

That fall, Evers enrolled at Alcorn A&M College in Lorman, Mississippi, where he completed high school and college under the GI Bill. (The federal Servicemen's Readjustment Act of 1944—better known as the GI Bill—paid for the education of returning World War II veterans. The bill also provided veterans with loans to help buy houses and start businesses.)

In college, Medgar Evers met Myrlie Beasley, an education major, and the two were married on Christmas Eve 1951. Although Myrlie Evers hoped to leave Mississippi for the north after college, Medgar wanted to stay in the state where he had been born. He believed that life for African Americans could improve there. He believed that he could help to transform his home state.

So Medgar and Myrlie stayed and raised their family in Mississippi. He would become a leader in the struggle for equal rights for African-American citizens. He would die for that cause.

Working for the NAACP

After college, Medgar Evers landed a job as an insurance salesman with one of the few black-owned companies in Mississippi. In his travels around the state, he saw the worst of African-American living conditions. The poverty of black sharecroppers was worse than anything he had seen before.

Evers was more determined than ever to bring about change. He joined the National Association for the Advancement of Colored People (NAACP) and tried to get others to join. But between 1889 and 1945, 13 percent of the country's 3,786 lynchings had taken place in Mississippi.[4] The NAACP barely existed there.

In 1953, Medgar Evers decided to take a bolder step. To his wife's horror, he announced his plans at an NAACP meeting. He would become the first African American to try to enter the University of Mississippi ("Ole Miss").

Evers's application to the university's law school was eventually rejected on a technicality. Even so, his bold move made the headlines of Jackson's *Daily News*. That drew attention to Evers as a civil rights activist.

At that time, the NAACP had field secretaries working in other states, building membership and reporting civil rights violations. However, Mississippi had long been considered too difficult and dangerous for such activities.

In 1954, the NAACP decided it was time to hire a field secretary for Mississippi.

Medgar Evers applied for the position. He was hired, and he spent the next seven years working from his office in the state capital of Jackson.

Medgar Evers at his typewriter, photographed in the early 1960s. He became the NAACP field secretary for Mississippi in 1954.

Evers also traveled 13,000 miles in his first year at work. He drove to small towns all over the state, trying to uncover the truth behind violent white-supremacist crimes. He was often alone, isolated both physically and emotionally. Even his black neighbors were afraid to associate with him.

The NAACP was a cautious national organization and slow to challenge white supremacy in Mississippi. Evers tried to move them along faster, and they tried to keep him in check. Although he was an engaging speaker, some considered his idealism and optimism naive.

By the late 1950s, the NAACP leadership realized that Evers had the ability to move an audience. They began sending him to other parts of the country to speak. From those other states, some of his speeches were televised.

By the time he returned home from the war, Medgar Evers was ready for a different kind of battle—one against Jim Crow laws in the South.

Perhaps Evers's greatest challenge was to overcome the fear of his own people. In the Deep South, African Americans had faced years of violent retaliation for any form of protest. Many were afraid to even meet with an NAACP leader, much less join the organization. They were well aware that some white people saw any gathering of blacks as a threat.

The African-American community had reasons to be afraid, and those reasons were the other part of Medgar Evers's jobs. Southern juries generally refused to convict white people accused of killing blacks. Evers not only

◻◻◻◻◻◻◻◻◻◻◻◻◻◻◻◻◻◻◻◻◻◻◻◻◻◻◻◻◻◻◻◻◻

investigated but also reported on racial brutalities. He saw to it that these cases were publicized so they would not go by unnoticed.

Threats and Brutalities

In 1954, the U.S. Supreme Court found that the idea of "separate but equal" education had not worked. In the case *Brown* v. *Board of Education,* the Court ordered that schools must be desegregated. In the South, that order—and any other movement toward integration—was met with increasing violence. The intimidation of African Americans reached a new high.

In 1955, Medgar Evers investigated the death of Emmett Till. The fourteen-year-old African American boy from Chicago had been visiting an uncle in the town of Money, Mississippi. It was claimed that Till had whistled at (or otherwise insulted) a white woman in a local store. Four days after that incident, a group of men kidnapped Till from his uncle's house, brutally beat him, shot him, and threw his weighted body into the Tallahatchie River.

Evers and other NAACP workers searched for information about Till's disappearance. After the body was found, they worked to locate black witnesses to the killing. Then, after the trial, they helped those witnesses slip out of town to escape retaliation.

When Till's body was returned to Chicago for burial, northern newspapers printed photographs of the teenager's mutilated corpse. National newspapers reported on the trial and the quick acquittal of the accused. It was the first Mississippi lynching to get such wide publicity. (After their acquittal, both of the accused men admitted to the crime.)

That same year, Evers reported on two African Americans who were killed after trying to vote and enroll others to vote. No arrests were made in that case. The local sheriff insisted that lead pellets in the corpse of a man killed with two shotgun blasts in the face were dental fillings.[5]

Clearly, in a time and place where such atrocities happened, Medgar Evers himself faced constant danger. He was beaten by white thugs on a bus, harassed, and threatened. In 1961, Evers attended the trial of African Americans arrested for a sit-in (a type of protest in which the participants sat down in a place reserved for whites). When he applauded the defendants, a nearby policeman hit him with a snub-nosed revolver.

That same year, Evers was charged and convicted of contempt of court. He had publicly criticized the conviction of a black man found guilty of burglary. Evers was fined one hundred dollars and sentenced to thirty days in jail, but the Mississippi Supreme Court overturned his conviction. Even though they disagreed with Evers's opinion, the court recognized his right to freedom of speech.

During 1962, racial tensions grew worse in Mississippi. That October, riots broke out on the University of Mississippi campus when James Meredith became the first black student to enroll there. Threats against Medgar Evers increased. He told a CBS interviewer about one particular telephone call. He had heard the cylinder of a revolver clicking on the other

Medgar Evers interviewing Beulah Melton, the wife of a shooting victim. As NAACP field secretary, Evers investigated violence against African Americans.

end of the line. The caller said, "This is for you." Evers replied, "Well, whenever my time comes, I'm ready."[6]

Evers did take some precautions. A 1962 visitor reported Evers answering the door with a gun in hand. Inside, furniture was piled in front of windows, and guns were placed in the living room and kitchen.[7]

In 1963, a firebomb exploded in the their carport. Over the years, Medgar Evers had grown somewhat more bitter and certainly more weary. Myrlie commented that shortly before his death, "he had aged ten years in the past two months."[8] Why did he not leave Mississippi? In answering that question, Evers said, "I may be going to heaven or hell, but I'll be going from Jackson."[9]

After the Murder

On June 13, 1963, *The New York Times* reported:

> A sniper lying in ambush shot and fatally wounded a Negro civil rights leader early today.
>
> The slaying touched off mass protests by Negroes in which 158 were arrested. It also aroused widespread fear of further racial violence in this state capital.[10]

In Jackson, Mississippi, four hundred young African Americans rioted, throwing bricks and bottles at the police. "Shoot us, shoot us!" the young people cried over and over again. No one fired on them, but the assassination ignited activism in the black community.

On June 15, an estimated three to four thousand people attended Medgar Evers's funeral. Onlookers and marchers shouted, "After Medgar, No More Fear."

Evidence and witness accounts soon pointed to Byron De La Beckwith. He was a prominent member of

"I'll Be Going From Jackson"

In the movie, Medgar Evers dies as the story begins, so we do not hear him speaking this line. In a conversation with Bobby DeLaughter, early in the movie, Myrlie Evers says that she said to Medgar, "Let's get out of Mississippi." She quotes his reply, "I don't know whether I'm going to heaven or to hell, but I'm going from Jackson."

In a made-up scene later in the movie, Bobby DeLaughter signals that he will continue the investigation by saying, "I don't know if I'm going to heaven or hell, but I'm going from Jackson."

two white-supremacist organizations, the Ku Klux Klan and the White Citizens' Council. While the secretive Klan was known for violent action, the White Citizens' Council strove to present a more respectable image. They said they were merely acting to maintain Southern customs—specifically, the custom of segregation.

The FBI made the first move against Beckwith, arresting him for violating Medgar Evers's civil rights. (That was a federal charge; murder had to be a state charge.) When Mississippi brought state murder charges, the FBI dropped out and left the prosecution in local hands.

A July 3, 1963, Associated Press article in *The New York Times* announced:

> The Hinds County grand jury indicted Byron de La Beckwith today for the murder of Medgar W. Evers, Negro civil rights leader. . . .

29

Evidence against Mr. Beckwith, a 42-year-old fertilizer salesman, was presented to the 18-member grand jury in secret session during the morning. . . .

Mr. Beckwith was arrested in his hometown, Greenwood, two weeks ago. He was charged by the Jackson City police with the slaying of Mr. Evers after the Federal Bureau of Investigation traced a rifle fingerprint to Mr. Beckwith.

In another civil rights development today, Charles Evers, brother of Medgar Evers, said that he received a threat on his life last night. Mr. Evers, state secretary for the N.A.A.C.P., said the threat was one of several since he took his brother's place in the desegregation movement.[11]

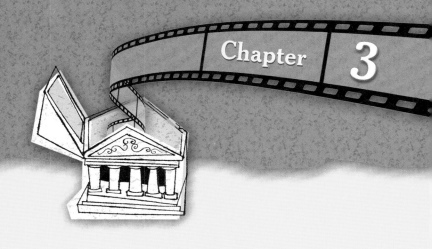

Chapter 3

Hung Juries

On that fateful night in June 1963, Myrlie Evers watched a speech on television as she waited for her husband to come home. President John F. Kennedy spoke to the nation about civil rights. At that time, many parts of the United States were in turmoil over challenges to segregation. During 1963 the arguments had become more violent.

In April, Martin Luther King, Jr., was arrested and jailed during antisegregation protests in Alabama. In May, the police commissioner, Eugene "Bull" Connor, used brutal force against nonviolent protestors in Birmingham, Alabama. On June 11, Alabama governor

George Wallace refused to allow two black students to enroll in the state university. Also on June 11, Martin Luther King, Jr., announced plans for a civil rights march to the nation's capital.

President Kennedy called up the Mississippi National Guard to help with the university crisis. (In an emergency situation, the National Guard unit that serves in a specific state can be mobilized by presidential order.)

In his speech that evening, Kennedy said:

> We are confronted primarily with a moral issue. It is as old as the scriptures and is as clear as the American Constitution.
>
> The heart of the question is whether all Americans are to be afforded equal rights and equal opportunities, whether we are going to treat our fellow Americans as we want to be treated. . . .
>
> We face, therefore, a moral crisis as a country and as a people.[1]

Medgar Evers was murdered just hours after Kennedy's speech, in the early minutes of July 12. A week later, President Kennedy proposed a civil rights bill to Congress. Kennedy was himself assassinated on November 22, 1963, in Dallas, Texas. The following year, at the urging of President Lyndon Johnson, Congress approved the Civil Rights Act as a memorial to the murdered president.

The entire nation was struggling with the moral issues that Kennedy spoke of, and no place more so than Mississippi. To many in the civil rights movement, the 1964 trials of Byron De La Beckwith for the murder of Medgar Evers were about the culture itself.

Mourners march to the funeral home in Jackson, Mississippi, for the funeral of Medgar Evers. It is estimated that three to four thousand people attended the service.

The Accused

Byron De La Beckwith VI—widely known as DeLay—
was born in California in 1920, but he grew up in
Greenwood, Mississippi. His father died when he was
five, and his mother died when he was eleven. DeLay
was raised by an uncle and two of his mother's male
cousins, none of whom wanted to take care of a child.
The adults disciplined DeLay severely, often beating him
with a belt.

Although he was a poor student, Beckwith finished
high school. He spent a few months at Mississippi State
College. A week after the December 7, 1941, Japanese
attack on the United States at Pearl Harbor, he joined
the army. During World War II, he was wounded in the
thigh during fighting in the Pacific.

DeLay Beckwith loved to talk, and he became a
successful fertilizer salesman. He did not seem like an
extremist to most people who met him. A former
employer commented, "I don't think he's any different
from any of the other old boys around here."[2]

Beckwith had a particular interest in firearms. Two
early childhood snapshots showed him with guns, and
as an adult he collected and traded guns. The police
soon discovered that Beckwith owned the rifle that had
killed Medgar Evers.

Beckwith was also known to be a racist. The 1954
Supreme Court decision on school desegregation infuri-
ated him. He was further fired up by racist speeches,
especially one given by Mississippi Circuit Court judge
Tom Brady, who had published a handbook calling the
day of the Supreme Court decision "Black Monday."[3]

The white-supremacist movement seemed to give Beckwith's life new meaning. White supremacists believe that Caucasian people are superior to those of other races. The Ku Klux Klan and similar organizations are white-supremacist groups. They claim that white people have the natural or God-given right to dominate other races.

Such thinking often causes xenophobia—the dislike or even hatred of people from other countries, cultures, ethnic groups, or races. Xenophobia has led to millions of murders all over the world. In Nazi Germany during World War II, the idea of "Aryan" superiority led to the attempted extermination of all those considered inferior, especially Jews.

Byron De La Beckwith began to identify himself as being forcefully against integration. He became a charter member of the White Citizens' Council, a white-supremacist group. In an article for the council's monthly newspaper, Beckwith wrote: "The Citizens' Council is the catalyst which set off the chain reaction which can save this Nation from mongrelization, totali-tarianism and judicial dictatorship."[4] By the end of the 1950s, the council had more than eighty thousand members in Mississippi.[5]

In 1956, Beckwith wrote to Mississippi governor J. P. Coleman, asking for a place on a new state commis-sion. The Sovereignty Commission was a state agency formed to block any move toward integration. Funded with taxpayer money, from 1956 to 1973 the commission fought against the civil rights movement. Their activities remained highly secret until the late 1980s.

In his letter of application to the Sovereignty Commission, Beckwith described himself as "rabid" about segregation. He also pointed out that he was "expert with a pistol, good with a rifle and fair with a shotgun."[6]

He did not receive an appointment to the Sovereignty Commission, so Beckwith carried on his own campaign. He wrote letters to politicians, church leaders, and newspapers about the importance of racial segregation. He sold copies of Brady's "Black Monday" speech. He even gave out segregationist handbills that he had printed at his own expense.

The white-supremacist movement seemed to give Byron De La Beckwith's life new meaning. He described himself as "rabid" about segregation.

The First Two Trials

After Medgar Evers's murder, detectives searched the area where they thought the gunman had stood. They found a 1917 .30-06 Enfield rifle hidden in nearby honeysuckle vines. Detectives photographed the gun and checked it for fingerprints.

The rifle appeared to have been wiped off after its use, but they found a single print on the scope. That fingerprint belonged to Byron De La Beckwith.[7] Beckwith admitted owning the rifle, but said that it had been stolen a week or so before the murder. He had just not gotten around to reporting the theft.

In 1964, Beckwith was tried twice for the murder of Medgar Evers, both times before all-white, all-male juries. His main defense lawyer was Hardy Lott, an associate from the White Citizens' Council. District Attorney Bill Waller prosecuted the case both times. Although Waller found several white witnesses who testified against Beckwith, no one could definitely place him at the scene of the crime.

Three policemen from Greenwood, Mississippi, sixty miles away, testified for Beckwith. They claimed that he had not even been in Jackson on the night of the murder. They testified under oath that DeLay Beckwith had been in Greenwood with them that night.

"Don't See That Every Day of the Week"

The movie *Ghosts of Mississippi* dramatizes the ex-governor's appearance by showing Myrlie Evers on the witness stand during Barnett's visit. Two characters, apparently reporters, explain what is happening:

> 1st REPORTER: Who's that?

> 2nd REPORTER: Ross Barnett.

> 1st REPORTER: You're kidding.

> 2nd REPORTER: Nope. Don't see that every day of the week. Former governor shaking hands with an accused assassin right in front of the jury.

> 1st REPORTER: There's not a court in America that would stand for that.

> 2nd REPORTER: What's America got to do with anything? This is Mississippi.

Beckwith had a lot of supporters in the white community who donated generously to his defense fund. Near the end of the February trial, powerful Mississippi ex-governor Ross Barnett walked into the courtroom. The man whose term had just ended in January shook Beckwith's hand. In full view of the jury, Beckwith and Barnett chatted amiably for about five minutes.

The first trial of Byron De La Beckwith for the murder of Medgar Evers ended with a hung jury in February 1964 and was declared a mistrial. Beckwith's second trial ended in April, with the same result—a hung jury, therefore a mistrial. The jury for the first trial had voted 7−5 for acquittal, the second jury had been evenly divided.

Charges against Beckwith were dropped in 1969. Those two trials would probably have been the end of the matter if Medgar Evers's widow had not been so persistent for so long.

What Is a Hung Jury, and Why Does It Cause a Mistrial?

In a criminal case, all jurors must agree on the verdict. When a jury in a criminal case cannot reach a unanimous verdict, it is called a "hung jury." When no verdict can be reached, the judge declares a mistrial, meaning that the defendant has been found neither innocent nor guilty.

Byron De La Beckwith, photographed at the beginning of his first trial. Beckwith's white-supremacist supporters donated money for his defense.

Myrlie Evers

Growing up in Vicksburg, Mississippi, Myrlie Beasley had a quiet childhood. She was raised by her grandmother and an aunt, both schoolteachers, so it seemed natural for Myrlie to follow in their paths when she enrolled in Alcorn A&M College. She planned to major in education and minor in music.

Her first day at college changed Myrlie's plans. She met Medgar Evers—an army veteran, an upperclassman, and a member of the football team. After the two were married, Myrlie Evers did not continue in school. When her husband became Mississippi state field secretary for the NAACP, she worked as his secretary.

Although Myrlie Evers participated in her husband's civil right activities, she feared for his life. In an interview for *Ebony* magazine, she said:

> We lived with death as a constant companion 24 hours a day. . . . Medgar knew what he was doing, and he knew what the risks were. He just decided that he had to do what he had to do. But I knew at some point in time he would be taken from me.[8]

Not only was her husband taken from her, but she had to watch his killer walk free.

After the two trials, Myrlie Evers moved her family to California. She went back to school at Pomona College in Claremont, and in 1968, she graduated with a sociology degree. She worked as assistant director of planning and development for the Claremont College system, then as consumer affairs director for the Atlantic Richfield Company in Los Angeles.

In 1975, Myrlie Evers married her second husband, Walter Williams. In June 1988, Los Angeles mayor Tom

Bradley appointed Myrlie Evers-Williams to the city's five-member Board of Public Works. She was the first African-American woman to hold such a powerful position in Los Angeles.

Although her life was busy and fulfilling, Myrlie Evers-Williams still visited Mississippi from time to time. She never gave up searching for new evidence concerning the murder of Medgar Evers. In 1989, she heard that new witnesses might come forward if there was another trial. Several people said they could testify that Beckwith had been in Jackson, not in Greenwood, on the night of the murder.

However, Myrlie Evers-Williams had a hard time arousing anyone's interest in reopening this old case. Many years had passed, and the courts had twice failed to convict the accused murderer. Of course, the courts had not acquitted Byron De La Beckwith, either. But Beckwith was now seventy-three years old, and most of the records and evidence used in the 1964 trials were missing.

New News About the Old Case

By the late 1980s, attitudes about race had changed in Mississippi. Although hard-core white supremacists like Byron De La Beckwith had not altered their views, many other citizens had. For example, Mississippi now had more elected black officials than any other state. Some citizens wanted to correct past mistakes and clean up Mississippi's image.

In 1989, a young red-haired reporter named Jerry Mitchell covered the courthouse beat for the Jackson *Clarion-Ledger* newspaper.[9] He also wrote a series of articles about racial strife during the 1960s. Mitchell got interested in the activities of a state commission that Beckwith had once applied to join.

When the Mississippi Sovereignty Commission had been shut down in the early 1970s, the state had sealed its records. Even so, Jerry Mitchell had found some Sovereignty Commission records that were not locked away. In 2002, he explained on the PBS *NewsHour*:

> I got interested in the Mississippi Sovereignty Commission, which was a State segregationist spy agency, and I got a tip that there were some Sovereignty Commission files which were sealed, but some of the files had supposedly been accidentally filed in an open-court file. So I went, and sure enough there they were, and I did a story about that, and that [piqued] my interest. And then that led me to find out about the Sovereignty Commission's involvement in the Medgar Evers case. . . .
>
> Well, basically I found out that at the same time that the State of Mississippi was prosecuting Byron De La Beckwith for the killing of Medgar Evers, this other arm of the State Sovereignty Commission, which was headed by the governor, was secretly assisting the defense in trying to get Beckwith acquitted.[10]

On Sunday, October 1, 1989, Mitchell's *Clarion-Ledger* article about Sovereignty Commission activities was published. On the following Tuesday, he wrote that Myrlie Evers-Williams had requested that the case against Byron De La Beckwith be reopened.

Soon the Hinds County district attorney's office received demanding calls and letters. Some insisted that because so many years had passed and the accused man was now elderly, the case should be left alone.

Others wanted immediate action for a new trial. Public opinion was divided and quite passionate on both sides.

Grounds for a New Trial?

When the uproar began, District Attorney Ed Peters and Assistant DA Bobby DeLaughter assumed that it would all blow over. After all, this case had been brought up several times over the years. Always before, interest had soon died down. It seemed to them that Mitchell wanted the case reopened without new evidence.

But this time, the public did not lose interest in the old murder. Bobby DeLaughter began to read Mitchell's newspaper stories with greater interest. He soon saw a possible reason to reopen the investigation.

Mitchell suggested that the Sovereignty Commission had tried to control who served on the jury for the first trial. If that were true, it could be grounds for a new trial. DeLaughter decided to look into whether the case against Beckwith could be reopened on the basis of jury tampering.

The assistant DA put an investigator to work tracking down jurors from the 1964 trials. R. D. "Doc" Thaggard was a quiet, unhurried, efficient man of few words.[11] He managed to locate and interview eleven of the twelve jurors from the second trial. But no one said they had ever been approached by the Sovereignty Commission.

In December 1989, DeLaughter reached the painful conclusion that he could not use the charge of jury tampering to reopen the case. The Sovereignty Commission might have been unethical in their close attention to jury selection, but he could not show that they had done anything illegal.

Medgar Evers's family at his funeral, with Darrell and Reena Evers seated next to their mother. Myrlie Evers moved her family to California after Beckwith's first two trials.

By that time, DeLaughter was unwilling to drop the case. The image of a hidden sniper, of a man dying in front of his wife and children, haunted his thoughts. Beckwith's own words haunted the young assistant district attorney too.

District Attorney Ed Peters had given DeLaughter a letter that Beckwith had written in 1987. The question of a third trial had also come up that year, and Beckwith had written to thank Peters for not reopening the investigation then:

> Surely a 3rd trial of me would turn Jackson . . . into a huge "Roman Circus fiesta" filling the air and streets with the bitterness and blackness of beasts, topped off and stirred with a vast multitude of trash of the white variety . . .[12]

Beckwith added a reminder that he had originally been a native of California, but had moved to Mississippi. He also referred to the fact that Myrlie Evers had moved to Los Angeles with her children.

> California got rid of a dear little white child, and lo— in 1965 California fell "heir" to a drove of darkies from Mississippi as the Evers' ooozzzed into the Los Angeles area!!![13]

DeLaughter was shocked at Beckwith's ugly words. Those comments did not prove Beckwith to be a murderer, but they did boost Bobby DeLaughter's interest in finding evidence against the man.

Chapter 4

His Own Words

Byron De La Beckwith had always been a talker. Although he continued to deny publicly that he had killed Evers, he did say that he was glad it had happened. As the years went by, Beckwith bragged to close friends that he had gotten away with the murder. He seemed to think that made him a very important man.

In 1989, Beckwith was living in Signal Mountain, Tennessee. He kept on talking and writing. His words spewed out hatred toward African Americans, Jews, and anyone who did not agree with him.

The Assistant District Attorney

Like Byron De La Beckwith, Assistant DA Bobby DeLaughter grew up in a segregated Mississippi. Born in

1954, he was a young boy when Medgar Evers was shot, and he did not even notice the event at that time. Bobby's life had little connection with that of African Americans.

Like other white students, he studied Mississippi history from textbooks that barely mentioned segregation, much less white supremacists or the Ku Klux Klan. When integration came to Bobby's school system in 1969, it was something of a surprise to him. But, unlike many adults in his community, he did not view desegregation as a crisis.

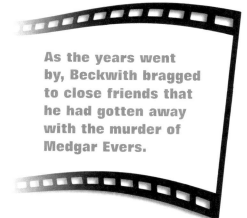

As the years went by, Beckwith bragged to close friends that he had gotten away with the murder of Medgar Evers.

When he was a senior at Wingfield High School in Jackson, the student body was 5 percent African American. Although sports programs went on as usual, the school administration had canceled extracurricular activities such as clubs and dances. But Bobby felt that racial integration "wasn't that big a deal."[1] To him, the problems existed more in the minds of the adults than among the students. As president of the student body, Bobby lobbied for a school-wide integrated prom, which was approved and held without any problems.

That did not mean that DeLaughter dedicated himself to civil rights causes. He pursued a career in the law, and at age nineteen he married Dixie Claire Townsend. She was the stepdaughter of Russel Moore, a judge who had been a militant segregationist during the 1960s. Bobby DeLaughter practiced law as a defense attorney for ten years. In 1987, he became a prosecutor in the district attorney's office.

In October 1989, DeLaughter began investigating the murder of Medgar Evers. Unlike Beckwith, he was known to be a man of few words. DeLaughter was serious while working and did not joke much in court. He described himself as "organized, methodical, and research-wise."[2]

DeLaughter was also persistent. During his prosecution of the case against Beckwith, he would keep going in spite of threats, attacks, and the breakup of his marriage.

Missing Evidence

In order to bring Byron De La Beckwith to trial again, the prosecutors had to first convince a grand jury that their request was reasonable. DeLaughter and his investigators began their search for enough evidence to make a third trial possible.

From court documents, they learned that a 1962 white Plymouth Valiant with a whiplike antenna had been spotted in a nearby parking lot on the night of the murder. Beckwith had owned a car fitting that description. The murder weapon had been found hidden in bushes, and Beckwith's fingerprints had turned up on the weapon. But where was all that evidence now?

Although DeLaughter searched a dusty storage warehouse for the files from the first trials, he came up empty-handed. So did everyone else who searched for records and evidence used in the first trials. In

November 1989, the Hinds County Courthouse clerk wrote a note to the district attorney:

> Dear Mr. Peters:
>
> After a diligent search of our evidence vault and inquiring with retired employees of this office, I have been unable to locate any evidence dealing with [the Beckwith case].[3]

The Investigation Continues

The DA's office had other work to handle besides the Evers murder, and Doc Thaggard was reassigned. DeLaughter continued his inquiries with investigators Lloyd "Benny" Bennett and Charles Morris Crisco, but

People outside the home of Medgar Evers shortly after the shooting. Evidence collected the night of the crime was not easy to find many years later.

they all had to double up on other cases at the same time.

Charlie Crisco was retired from the Homicide Division of the Jackson Police Department. After the *Clarion-Ledger* reported that the Mississippi Sovereignty Commission had been involved in the Beckwith case, Crisco showed up to work as an investigator. The wiry detective had an excellent reputation from his years with the police force.

Benny Bennett was a detective with the Jackson Police Department, on loan to the DA's office as an investigator. Bennett became intensely interested in the case when he recognized a face in an old photograph of the 1964 crime team. "That's my daddy," he commented.[4] Benny was eager to finish up the job his father had started.

In March 1990, the *Clarion-Ledger* located the two Greenwood policemen who had testified that Beckwith had been with them the night of the murder. Although

Benny Bennett as Benny Bennett

Lloyd "Benny" Bennett was still a police officer and investigator in Jackson, Mississippi, when Rob Reiner, the director, was there shooting *Ghosts of Mississippi*. When Reiner offered Benny the chance to play himself in the film, the officer took the part. Actor William H. Macy, who played Charlie Crisco, later wrote a character for Bennett to play in his 1998 movie *The Con*.

they stuck with their story, DeLaughter considered their testimony highly suspect. If they had known that Beckwith could not have killed Evers, why had they let him sit in jail for eight months before they came forward as witnesses?

The police photographer discovered the official 1963 crime scene photographs in a box stuck away in the bottom of a closet. Among the photos were shots of Beckwith's Plymouth Valiant with the whiplike antenna. When enlarged with modern methods, one picture clearly showed a Shriner's emblem on the car—exactly as a witness had described it on the car parked near the crime scene. That meant Beckwith's car had been in Jackson the night of the murder, not in Greenwood.

In May 1990, *Clarion-Ledger* reporter Jerry Mitchell showed up at DeLaughter's office. Mitchell had published some stories about possible witnesses that the DA's office wanted kept secret. So none of the investigators were eager to chat with him. But Mitchell was there to help. He pulled out a binder titled *State of Mississippi* v. *Byron De La Beckwith*. DeLaughter was stunned. He had made a huge, futile search for this very document—the transcript of Beckwith's first trial.

Back in the sixties, Myrlie Evers had heard that the Mississippi Sovereignty Commission was taking all documents related to the murder, so she had stored the transcript away for safekeeping. She had recently given Jerry Mitchell this copy of her original. Although Bobby DeLaughter had often talked with Evers-Williams, she had never mentioned having the transcript. Clearly, he had not gained her complete confidence.

The Murder Weapon and the Mistake

DeLaughter's investigators relocated the man who had traded the gun to Beckwith. The crime-scene photos showed the fingerprint found on the gun and its comparison with Beckwith's fingerprint. The photos also included details of the rifle that had fired the assassin's bullet. But that murder weapon was still missing.

DeLaughter remembered a comment made by a former court clerk, suggesting that the judge might have kept the rifle. Apparently it had not been unusual for judges to keep souvenirs from a trial. Looking at the photographs, DeLaughter began to remember seeing an old rifle like that somewhere.

His own father-in-law, a judge, had once showed him a gun that he said was from a civil rights case. Although

Why Was the Transcript So Important?

A transcript is an official word-for-word written record of the testimony taken in a trial or hearing. It contains the exact words of witnesses and describes the evidence presented.

The prosecutor could use the transcript to help relocate all the original evidence and witnesses. He could also tell what was left out of the earlier trials. Although DeLaughter would need the original official transcript for the actual indictment and trial, he could put Evers-Williams's copy to good use in his investigation.

his father-in-law had not been the presiding judge in Beckwith's trial, could the gun have passed into his hands? Indeed, DeLaughter found the rifle in his father-in-law's collection. The serial number matched the one in police records—the serial number of the murder weapon.

Then the young assistant DA and his team made a mistake. DeLaughter did not want the news to get out that they had found the murder weapon. So he did not log the gun into evidence, and the investigators kept the discovery secret.

That June, Jerry Mitchell confronted Bobby DeLaughter. A reliable source, who turned out to be DeLaughter's brother-in-law, had told reporters that the DA's office had the gun. The next day's newspaper headlines proclaimed that the prosecutors had withheld evidence and lied to the press. The story soon progressed to television.

Myrlie Evers-Williams's confidence in DeLaughter was badly shaken. During all these years, she had found little reason to trust those who claimed they were investigating the murder of her husband. Discovering that the gun had not been entered into evidence made her suspicious of DeLaughter. She still had not told him that she had the official trial transcript.

Discovering New Evidence

Even though the investigators had relocated most of the old evidence from the early trials, it would not be enough. They would also need something new to get an indictment.

A lawyer friend contacted DeLaughter about an out-of-print book titled *Klandestine*. Several men said to be Klansmen were suing Orion Pictures over their portrayals in the film *Mississippi Burning*. In his research to defend Orion, the lawyer had come across this book that told the story of an informant for the FBI on Ku Klux Klan activities. It quoted Beckwith bragging in typical fashion when he was the speaker at a Klan rally:

> Killing that nigger gave me no more inner discomfort than our wives endure when they give birth to our children. We ask them to do that for us. We should do just as much. So, let's get in there and kill those enemies, including the President, from the top down![5]

DeLaughter tracked down the FBI informant, Delmar Dennis, who became one of the new witnesses before the grand jury. Other witnesses came forward to say they had seen Beckwith in Jackson on the night of the murder. They had not spoken up at the earlier trials because they had not believed that their testimonies would do any good.

By this time, Bobby DeLaughter was keeping Myrlie Evers-Williams well-informed about the progress of

Not in the Movie

The movie *Ghosts of Mississippi* does not include the copy of the transcript that Jerry Mitchell brought to Bobby DeLaughter. It only shows the official transcript being given to DeLaughter by Myrlie Evers-Williams.

Members of the white-supremacist Ku Klux Klan terrorized African Americans. Byron De La Beckwith bragged at a Klan rally about killing Medgar Evers.

the investigation. On October 12, 1990, she brought her transcript of the first trial to him. It was *the* official transcript—three volumes totaling some two hundred thousand words—given to her by District Attorney Waller after the second mistrial. The court authenticated the transcript on November 19.

In December 1990, DeLaughter presented his case against Byron De La Beckwith to a grand jury. Then he and Myrlie Evers-Williams waited anxiously as the jurors deliberated. They needed at least twelve of the eighteen jurors to agree to indict Beckwith again.

One juror voted no, because she believed that too much time had gone by since the crime was committed. But seventeen jurors—more than enough—voted for reindictment! On December 14, 1990, a Mississippi grand jury indicted Byron De La Beckwith for the third and final time for the murder of Medgar Evers.

Challenges and Delays

On December 17, 1990, Byron De La Beckwith was arrested in Tennessee and charged for the 1963 murder of Medgar Evers. Bobby DeLaughter described what followed as "three years of legal calisthenics."[6] Myrlie Evers-Williams began to despair that another trial would ever take place.

Beckwith was at first denied bail, but eight months later he was released on a $100,000 bond. The lawyers assigned to him by the court fought his extradition to Mississippi for trial. When a judge ruled against them, they brought new motions alleging violations of Beckwith's right to a speedy trial. They also challenged a new trial on the basis of double jeopardy. Those last two issues went to the Mississippi Supreme Court, where the prosecution won the argument.

As the delays dragged on, Bobby DeLaughter and his team continued pulling together evidence for the trial they still hoped would come. They got a court order and exhumed the body of Medgar Evers, so they could offer new forensic testimony on the cause of death. They struggled to keep witnesses available.

The wait was especially hard on DeLaughter. His wife, Dixie, did not agree with him that the case should have been reopened. The long hours he spent on the investigation put an added strain on their relationship. They divorced in April 1991, after seventeen years of marriage. Bobby DeLaughter kept custody of their three children, Burt, Claire, and Drew.

DeLaughter also endured threats and attempted intimidation. One night, he got a phone call claiming that a bomb was about to go off in his house. In a panic, he rushed his children outside. Fortunately, the threat proved to be a hoax.

In July 1993, the U.S. Supreme Court refused to review the Beckwith case. The delays were finally over.

The Third Trial

On January 28, 1994, the third trial of Byron De La Beckwith began. District Attorney Ed Peters and Assistant DA Bobby DeLaughter worked together on the prosecution. They had the murder weapon, the telescopic sight with Beckwith's fingerprint on it, and many witnesses from the 1964 trials. Stand-ins read the words of witnesses who had since died. The jurors looked at the gun and handled the bullet fragments that had been taken from Evers's body.

There was little new evidence. With the enlarged photograph, the Plymouth Valiant in the parking lot could now be positively identified as belonging to Beckwith. Modern forensics proved that particular rifle to definitely be the murder weapon. Six new witnesses testified that Beckwith had bragged about killing Evers. Others testified to seeing Beckwith in Jackson on the night of the murder. Even so, they were recalling words and events from a long time ago.

New Witnesses to an Ugly Past

In the 1994 trial, six new witnesses testified that Beckwith had bragged about killing Medgar Evers.

- Mary Ann Adams of Mississippi said that she met Beckwith at a restaurant in 1966. He had come over to the table where she was sitting with a friend. He actually introduced himself as "Byron De La Beckwith, the man who killed Medgar Evers." When Adams refused to shake Beckwith's hand, he became angry. Believing that Beckwith could not be tried again, she had not told the law at that time. But she contacted DeLaughter when she learned that the case was being reopened.[7]

- Dan Prince of Tennessee had rented an apartment in Beckwith's home during the 1980s. One day, Beckwith had told Prince that he had been tried twice in Mississippi, "for killing that nigger. I had a job to do and I did it and I didn't suffer any more for it than my wife would when she was going to have a baby."[8]

- Elluard Jenoal "Dick" Davis of Florida had once been a member of the Ku Klux Klan. While remaining in the Klan, Davis became an FBI informant. In 1969, Davis had talked with Beckwith in a Florida restaurant. Beckwith had talked about his trial and bragged about the murder. Davis had reported that incident to the FBI.

- Peggy Morgan and her husband lived in Greenwood, Mississippi. One Sunday, the couple had given Beckwith a ride to the state penitentiary, where they were all visiting prisoners. Beckwith was going to see a Klan member who had been convicted of murdering former NAACP president Vernon Dahmer.

During the trip, Beckwith warned the Morgans about letting anyone know about his visit. Peggy Morgan testified that Beckwith said that "he had killed Medgar Evers, a nigger, and . . . he wasn't scared to kill again." Beckwith warned her that news of his visit to the penitentiary had better not get out.[9]

- Delmar Dennis of Tennessee was also a Klansman turned FBI informant. Dennis testified about a Klan rally on August 8, 1965. Beckwith had said he had not suffered from "killing that nigger." He had urged his audience to become more violent, to "kill from the top down."[10]

- On the fourth day of testimony, Mark Reiley became the last of thirty-five witnesses called by the prosecution. His story supported what the others had said. District Attorney Ed Peters later referred to Reiley as his "cleanup hitter."[11]

The Arguments

DeLaughter portrayed Beckwith as an avowed white supremacist "whose own venom had come back to

Movie Witnesses

Screenwriter Lewis Colick only included three of the six new witnesses at Beckwith's 1994 trial. They were Dan Prince, Peggy Morgan, and Delmar Dennis. Perhaps he felt that those testimonies brought up all the points that needed to be made.

haunt him."[12] He said that Beckwith had been proud of killing the NAACP's Mississippi field director. DeLaughter presented letters that Beckwith had written to several white-supremacist organizations after his 1963 trials. For example, in *Attack!* magazine, Beckwith wrote that he had been tried in 1963 for killing "Mississippi's mightiest nigger," and said there was still work to be done.

Byron De La Beckwith did not testify in his own behalf. Perhaps his lawyers felt that the defendant had already done enough talking.

Beckwith's attorneys included Jim Kitchens, who had previously been a prosecutor in southern Mississippi. Kitchens insisted that holes in the prosecution's case caused reasonable doubt. Kitchens reminded the jury that his client's views were not on trial. He reviewed the testimony of witnesses who said that Beckwith had been ninety-five miles and two hours away when Medgar Evers was shot.

Kitchens told the jury:

> Nobody can legally or morally question your verdict if you don't believe that the state's case has been proven without reasonable doubt. . . . We don't just do that for people we like and admire, but for everyone. And if Byron De La Beckwith can't get a fair trial, then no one can get a fair trial.[13]

Bobby DeLaughter closed the prosecution's argument with a challenge and a question: "On behalf of the State of Mississippi, I ask that you hold this defendant accountable. Find him guilty, simply because it's right, it's just, and Lord knows, it's just time. . . . Is it ever too late to do the right thing?"[14]

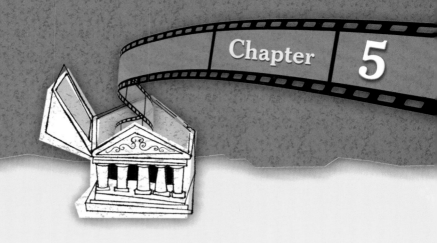

Chapter 5

Is It Ever Too Late?

After his closing statement, Bobby DeLaughter could not sit still in the courtroom for another moment. He went outside and paced the hallway, drinking coffee, while the defense gave their summation. In closing the case for the defense, attorney Merrida Coxwell said, "Byron De La Beckwith didn't kill Medgar Evers. We can't prove who did, but we are not required to."[1]

Finally the jury was escorted from the courtroom. They were to have lunch, then start their deliberations that afternoon. When the jury had failed to reach a decision by six-thirty that evening, they went to their hotel for the night. They would begin their work again at nine the next morning.

Bobby DeLaughter was worried. What could be hanging up this jury? If they had not reached a decision in the first five hours, was there any chance of a conviction? Would this be yet another mistrial? That night, a ferocious rainstorm hit Jackson, Mississippi. DeLaughter said he felt that "something cataclysmic was at hand—the day of reckoning."[2]

The Verdict

The next morning, February 5, 1994, the phone in the district attorney's office rang at 9:35. The jury had reached a verdict. DeLaughter rushed to the courtroom, where the judge held up the proceedings for a few minutes until Myrlie Evers arrived from her hotel.

The jury foreman, a black minister, handed the piece of paper to the court clerk. The clerk read aloud, "We, the jury, find the defendant guilty as charged." Deputies with walkie-talkies relayed the news to those in the hallway outside the courtroom, and soon cheers and applause rang through the building.

Byron De La Beckwith's wife, Thelma, cried out a protest that she had made many times in early Saturday morning phone calls to Bobby DeLaughter, "He's not guilty! . . . The Jews did it!"[3]

Judge Hilburn brought the now-subdued Byron De La Beckwith forward for sentencing. The judge said, "Mr. Beckwith, by mandate of the laws of the State of Mississippi, it is required that I sentence you to a term of life imprisonment."[4]

Myrlie Evers-Williams shouted a cheer and raised a fist in triumph. As DeLaughter slipped out of the courtroom by way of a back stairwell, she followed and hugged him.

"Thank you so much for me, my family, and for Medgar," Myrlie Evers-Williams said. "He can rest in peace now."[5]

DeLaughter felt a deep gratitude to the people who had contributed to the case throughout its long history: judges who had moved the case forward; brave witnesses who had risked testifying; detectives, investigators, district attorneys, and reporters who had gathered evidence; jurors who had the courage to vote guilty. Most of all, he was grateful to Myrlie Evers-Williams, who had never given up.

The 1994 jury was made up of seven women (five black) and five men (three black). This time, social attitudes were different from those of thirty years ago. This group of jurors believed the witnesses who quoted Beckwith's own words. This jury had no problem convicting a defendant who had bragged about killing a black man and getting away with it.

A Quicker Verdict

In the movie *Ghosts of Mississippi*, it seems that the jury reached their decision on the first day. We hear arguments from the jury room and see Myrlie Evers and Bobby DeLaughter talking together and waiting. There is no indication that the jury left for the night. Then the movie jumps to the jury's return.

Beckwith's lawyers appealed the verdict, again saying that the thirty-one-year lapse between the murder and the conviction had denied the defendant a fair trial. Even the chief justice of the Mississippi Supreme Court, Dan Lee, agreed with them. He felt that Beckwith's retrial had violated the defendant's rights, and that the conviction should be overturned.[6]

Nevertheless, the majority of the Mississippi Supreme Court rejected the appeal. In 1997, by a 4–2 vote, the court upheld the conviction of Byron De La Beckwith for the 1963 murder. He would spend the rest of his life in jail.

DeLaughter had been worried about the outcome of the appeal. He later described hearing the news: "Yes! Yes! Tears of joy trickled from the corners of my eyes, and I said a prayer of thanks."[7]

The Supreme Court judgment read in part:

> Miscreants brought before the bar of justice in this State must, sooner or later, face the cold realization that justice, slow and plodding though she may be, is certain in the State of Mississippi. . . . Final resolution of this conflict resulted from voices, both present and past, who showed the courage and will, from 1964 to 1994, to merely state the truth in open court. Their voices cannot be ignored. We affirm the finding of the jury that Byron De La Beckwith VI murdered Medgar Evers on the night of June 12, 1963.[8]

A New Funeral for Medgar Evers

In 1963, the murder of Medgar Evers had been mourned nationally. The slain civil rights leader had been buried in Arlington National Cemetery with full military honors

Myrlie Evers-Williams and her daughter Reena Evers-Everett celebrate the murder conviction of Byron De La Beckwith (top). The photo below shows the actress Whoopi Goldberg portraying the same moment.

"Thank you so much for me, my family, and for Medgar," Myrlie Evers-Williams said to Bobby DeLaughter. "He can rest in peace now."

before a crowd of thousands. In 1994, he would have another funeral.

His body, buried for twenty-eight years, had been exhumed for a new autopsy, and the testimony of the forensics expert was helpful in the new trial. When the casket had first been opened, those present were stunned at the body's perfect condition. DeLaughter described the moment, "A collective gasp sounded throughout the room. . . . Medgar Evers looked as if he had just been placed in the coffin."[9]

The forensic pathologist, Dr. Michael Baden, has consulted on many high-profile cases. He was also amazed at the excellent condition of Evers's body. He credited that to an excellent job of embalming at the funeral home and to the fact that the grave had been very deep. But he, like others present, felt that a scientific explanation alone could not account for the perfect condition of the body.

Van Evers, the youngest of Medgar Evers's children, had no memory of his father. The others had also been very young when their father was murdered. A second funeral was held for Medgar Evers, providing closure for his entire family.

Myrlie Evers-Williams

The widow of Medgar Evers did not stop working for civil rights causes. From 1995 to 1998 she served as chairwoman of the NAACP. She received honorary doctorates from seven colleges and universities. Her many awards include the U.S. Congressional Black Caucus Achievement Award and the League of Women Voters' Woman of Honor Award. She was named California Woman of the Year, and the NAACP also recognized her with an Image Award for Civil Rights.

Myrlie Evers's 1967 book, *For Us, the Living*, was made into a television drama starring Howard Rollins as Medgar Evers. In 1975, she met and married Walter Williams; he died from cancer in 1995. In 1999, she published an autobiography, *Watch Me Fly: What I Learned on the Way to Becoming the Woman I Was Meant to Be.*

When she was interviewed for the 1989 best seller *I Dream a World: Black Women Who Changed America,* Myrlie Evers-Williams said that she "greets today and the future with open arms."[10]

Beckwith in Jail

Journalist Adam Nossiter tried to interview Beckwith in jail in 1992, as he awaited trial. When the prisoner realized that Nossiter was Jewish, he shouted, "You're a damn Jew. Get out! Get out!"[11]

Soon afterward, Beckwith wrote to a relative about the incident:

> I just threw the snotty-nosed, 6' 4", yellow-skinned, mongrel, damned-by-God, stinking . . . Jew out of my comfortable chamber. . . .
>
> He's been writing an anti-Delay, anti-white, anti-Christian, anti-Dixie book. . . .[12]

His long years in prison did nothing to change DeLay Beckwith's opinions. He produced a constant flow of letters to fellow white supremacists, thanking those who supported him. He urged others to join his wife's campaign to get him pardoned. In 1995, when Beckwith claimed to be "President of the Confederate States of America," even his supporters suggested that he should have a mental evaluation. Beckwith rejected the notion.

In a 1999 letter to his son, Beckwith repeated his favorite phrase, "I will continue to fight on for all that is white, right and Christian—and I am glad to do that."[13] In January 2001, Byron De La Beckwith died of high blood pressure, heart trouble, and other health problems in the University of Mississippi Medical Center in Jackson at the age of eighty.

Beckwith's family and friends gave him an elaborate burial in Chattanooga, Tennessee. At the funeral, Beckwith's son, known as DeLay Jr., cried out again and again, "It ain't over, it ain't over."[14]

Bobby DeLaughter

On the long road to the third trial, Bobby DeLaughter met and married Peggy Lloyd, a nurse he still refers to as the love of his life. But DeLaughter's career did not go smoothly in the years immediately after the verdict against Beckwith.

DeLaughter had always wanted to be a judge. In 1993, Mississippi created a court of appeals. Five justices were to be chosen for the new court in the 1994 general elections. Bobby DeLaughter ran for one of those judgeships.

Byron De La Beckwith and his wife, Thelma, at the time of his last trial for the murder of Medgar Evers. Beckwith retained his segregationist views to the end.

At first, he felt confident about the election, but DeLaughter quickly discovered that many white citizens still resented his prosecution of Beckwith. He faced hard stares from men who refused to shake his hand. He faced women who threw his campaign literature back in his face. He lost the election by a wide margin.

DeLaughter wrote in his book *Never Too Late*:

> I should have seen it coming, but I didn't. I lost the election, clobbered, two to one.
>
> I was devastated, not because I had lost (after all, it was my inaugural political outing), but because the underlying reason was this one case. . . . I was also pierced to the core by those who didn't bother to vote. . . .[15]

DeLaughter noted that he was not the only one who paid a price for his involvement in the Beckwith case. His father lost several business clients across the state.

Why Did Bobby DeLaughter Have to Run in an Election to Become a Judge?

In general, judges can be chosen by public election or can be appointed by a public official or a higher judge. The Mississippi constitution specifies that judges are to be elected, but they can be appointed to fill the unexpired term of a judge who leaves office. The appointed judge must then compete in the next general election to hold that position.

Only after the 1996 release of the movie *Ghosts of Mississippi* did attitudes toward DeLaughter begin to change. Finally, "many people realized that our motives were not political and appreciated our efforts. Hardly a day goes by now without someone writing or telling me as much."[16]

In 1998, DeLaughter's closing argument in the Beckwith case was one of ten published in a best-selling volume, *Ladies & Gentlemen of the Jury: Greatest Closing Arguments in Modern Law.* In December 1999, he received a telephone call from the office of Mississippi governor Kirk Fordice. The governor was appointing DeLaughter to fill the unexpired term of a Hinds County judge who had recently died.

Bobby DeLaughter's longtime dream was finally coming true. On December 10, 1999, he took the oath of office in the same courtroom where all three of Byron De La Beckwith's trials had taken place.

In 2000, DeLaughter ran for reelection, and this time he won his judgeship with 80 percent of the vote. In 2002, he was unopposed for the position. He also served as president of the Mississippi Prosecutor's Association. His book *Never Too Late: A Prosecutor's Story of Justice in the Medgar Evers Case*, was published in 2001.

In a postscript written after he became a judge, Bobby DeLaughter observed, "Times do change, and life is good."[17]

Chapter 6

Ghosts of Mississippi

William Weaks Morris, known as Willie, was a Pulitzer Prize-winning author and a native of Jackson. He saw much of the 1994 trial of Byron De La Beckwith, and the courtroom drama deeply moved him. Fred Zollo, a friend of Morris's in the motion-picture business, also arrived Jackson at the end of the trial. Zollo was hoping to see the verdict.

Zollo could not get into the crowded courtroom. But Morris was present for the stunning moment when the jury found Beckwith guilty of murder. Morris reported on the trial in a magazine article entitled "Justice, Justice at Last."[1]

Morris also persuaded Zollo that the investigation and trial would make an inspiring movie. Zollo was the right person to approach about the project, as he had produced the civil rights drama *Mississippi Burning*. He quickly went to work turning the Medgar Evers case into a motion picture.

Castle Rock Entertainment production company hired screenwriter Lewis Colick to go to Jackson and begin researching the film. Colick found the Beckwith assignment daunting and time consuming. With journalistic dedication, he gathered about three hundred pages of information from research and interviews.

Zollo hired Rob Reiner, director of the romantic comedy *When Harry Met Sally* and the military courtroom drama *A Few Good Men*. Zollo and Reiner then assembled a group of stellar actors. Alec Baldwin was cast as Bobby DeLaughter, Whoopi Goldberg as Myrlie Evers-Williams, and James Woods as Byron De La Beckwith. All the leading actors felt an unusually deep commitment to the project.

The Pursuit of Realism

Director Rob Reiner wanted the movie to be as realistic as possible. He shot a great deal of *Ghosts of Mississippi* in Jackson and surrounding areas. Many scenes were filmed in and around the Hinds County Courthouse in Jackson, where all three trials of Byron De La Beckwith took place. While they were shooting, Beckwith remained in a jail cell in the courthouse. His lawyers were appealing the verdict.

Jackson residents experienced eerie moments when James Woods appeared on location as the elderly

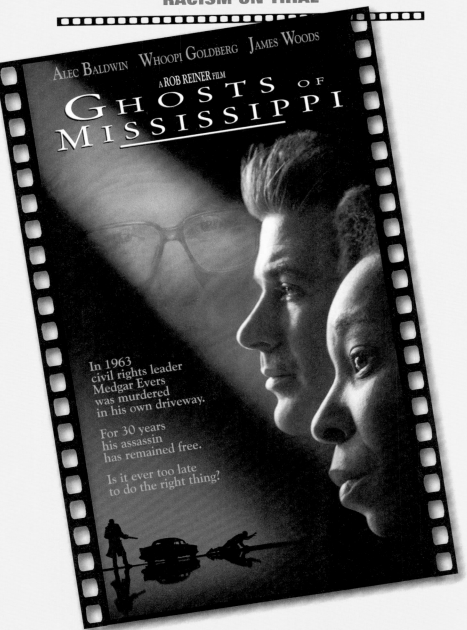

Ghosts of Mississippi, a film based on the efforts to bring Byron De La Beckwith to justice, opened in 1996.

Willie Morris's Movie "Appearance"

Fairly early in the movie *Ghosts of Mississippi*, Bobby DeLaughter and his wife, Dixie, are seen in bed reading. Bobby is studying legal materials, while Dixie is reading Willie Morris's book *North Toward Home*. If it had not been for Morris's influence on producer Fred Zollo, *Ghosts of Mississippi* might never have been made. Morris's 1998 book *The Ghosts of Medgar Evers* described the making of the film. He died in 1999.

Beckwith. Woods's makeup pioneered the use of gelatins to simulate old age. The result was an uncanny resemblance to Beckwith.[2] Woods's powerful acting, which earned him a 1997 Oscar nomination, created a vivid sense of Beckwith's hateful self-importance.

While Woods was filming the trial scenes, Bobby DeLaughter was startled by a newspaper photograph of the actor on the set and in character. DeLaughter almost mistook Woods for Beckwith.[3] The sight of Woods as Beckwith also shook up Myrlie Evers-Williams.

During a break on one day of shooting, Whoopi Goldberg complained to reporters that Beckwith was using taxpayers' money for postage to send out hate literature. At that moment, Woods approached her in makeup.

Playing Beckwith to perfection, he led Goldberg gallantly away from reporters. "I swear," he said, "if I'd met a woman like this in my prime, I'd [have] changed my views on segregation." A reporter described the moment as "too surreal for words, even for Hollywood."[4]

However, there were lengths to which even Woods would not go in pursuit of realism. Although Beckwith was in the same building during the shooting of the courtroom scenes, Woods refused to study him in person. He said:

> For one thing, he shot somebody else in the back in front of his wife and kids. There is no reason that could ever justify that kind of horrible behavior. So why would I want to meet him? I also didn't want to further glorify his inflated sense of himself. I wouldn't want to breathe the same air.[5]

However, the situation between Whoopi Goldberg and Myrlie Evers-Williams was very different. The actress had long admired Evers-Williams and had met her before the shooting of *Ghosts of Mississippi*. Goldberg talked often with Evers-Williams about the events dramatized in the movie. Evers-Williams told Goldberg how difficult it had been to overcome her hatred for all white people after her husband's murder.

Evers-Williams, credited as a consultant for the film, also helped shape the screenplay. As director Reiner put it, "We sent her every draft of the script and she gave us feedback and notes that I tried to incorporate as much as I could. Virtually everything that Whoopi says in the movie is something that Myrlie told us she'd said."[6]

In full makeup, the actor James Woods had an
uncanny resemblance to Byron De La Beckwith.

The Haunted Location

Several scenes were filmed at the former home of Myrlie Evers and her slain husband. These scenes included the murder itself. James Pickens Jr., who played the part of Medgar Evers, acted the moment of the shooting in the very spot where the real-life Evers was felled.

The cameras filmed the reenactment of the murder again and again. Medgar Evers's brother Charles, Bobby DeLaughter, and people who had lived in the neighborhood ever since the murder had occurred mingled among the crew. The neighbors gave valuable eyewitness advice, especially about how the mortally wounded Evers was taken away from the scene.

While filming the murder, Reiner worried about how Charles Evers was handling it. "Are you sure you want to be around here for this?" Reiner asked.

"I'll be OK," Charles replied.

Reiner later observed in an interview, "He was almost like a moth to a flame; he had to see it. It was like he was saying good-bye to his brother again." [7]

Bobby DeLaughter found it harrowing to watch the murder played out repeatedly. When the filming ended, Reiner asked DeLaughter if he thought the crew had gotten a good shot. DeLaughter later said to a reporter, "I told him that if feeling heartsick and angry all over again is a sign that this is a good shot, then it's a good shot." [8]

Dramatic Liberties

Director Rob Reiner explained:

> I felt a tremendous responsibility to make this film as accurate as possible. . . . We haven't deviated one iota from what happened in this case. Perhaps

people will think we made it up, as it is so astounding. But since many people now get their history through movies, I wanted to portray the characters in this film as honestly as we possibly could.[9]

Ghosts of Mississippi is, indeed, remarkably accurate in comparison with many other Hollywood "real life" stories. But probably every movie based on historical events has taken some liberties. *Ghosts of Mississippi* is no exception.

The Gun—in Real Life and on Film

One of the most dramatic developments in the actual case was the rediscovery of the long-missing murder weapon—Beckwith's Enfield .30-06.

In the movie, Bobby DeLaughter is talking with his little boy at home when the topic of guns comes up. It suddenly occurs to DeLaughter that his father-in-law, the late Judge Russel Moore, might have kept the gun as a souvenir. Already separated from his wife, Dixie, DeLaughter rushes his children to the home of his mother-in-law, Caroline. He interrupts a bridge game.

Startling Caroline's guests, DeLaughter barges upstairs into the judge's study. His alarmed mother-in-law follows him, knowing exactly what he is looking for. Defying Caroline's protests, DeLaughter searches the room. He quickly finds the gun in a wooden chest, checks the serial number, and sees that it matches the original. Beside himself with joy, he hugs the dismayed Caroline. Then he leaves the house as abruptly as he came.

In real life, the episode unfolded much less dramatically. As soon as DeLaughter realized where the gun might be, he called Caroline from his office. He explained his concern and asked for permission to look through her husband's gun collection. Caroline readily agreed to let him do so.

DeLaughter then called Dixie, from whom he had not actually yet separated. Although far from happy with DeLaughter's involvement in the case, she accompanied him to her mother's house. Their children were at the home of DeLaughter's mother and did not join them.

When DeLaughter and his wife arrived at the Moore home, Caroline graciously led them to where she kept what she called her late husband's "long guns." DeLaughter quickly found the weapon, and his mother-in-law allowed him to take it away with no protest.

Ghosts of Mississippi is remarkably accurate in comparison with many other Hollywood "real life" stories. But the movie took some liberties with historical events.

So in the scene, the filmmakers exaggerated family tensions to add suspense and humor. In scenes that followed, they also took liberties with Bobby DeLaughter's handling of the gun's discovery. In the movie, DeLaughter promptly and dutifully logs the gun into evidence. But he tells his colleagues that Myrlie Evers must not find out that he has found the weapon. She might let the information slip to reporter Jerry Mitchell, who would then put it in a newspaper story.

Alec Baldwin as Bobby DeLaughter and Whoopi Goldberg as
Myrlie Evers-Williams face a group of journalists outside the
courtroom in a scene from *Ghosts of Mississippi*.

This would be a disaster to the case, DeLaughter explains to his colleagues. He reminds them that Byron De La Beckwith is currently talking openly and rashly to anyone who will listen. Sooner or later, he is liable to say something self-incriminating. But if he learns that the gun has been found, he will know that the DA's office is serious about the case. Then he might shut up. It is far better, DeLaughter insists, to keep the gun's discovery a secret—especially from Myrlie Evers.

In reality, Bobby DeLaughter's actions and motives in handling the gun were more complicated. True, he was genuinely concerned that Myrlie Evers might leak the information to the press, silencing Beckwith's bluster. But he was also worried about embarrassing his family.

If the case went to trial, DeLaughter knew that he would have to reveal that he had found the gun in the home of his in-laws. But at that time, he also believed that the case might not go anywhere. If it did not, DeLaughter wrote in his book *Never Too Late*, "I would give the gun back to Carolyn to do with as she pleased, with nobody getting embarrassed."[10] In fact, DeLaughter did not (as in the movie) log the gun into evidence. He kept it in his house.

In the film, DeLaughter is willing to sacrifice even his family's feelings to the needs of the investigation. But DeLaughter admitted that his motives were not so pure, at least not when it came to dealing with the murder weapon. Subtle changes in the story kept movie audiences from being seriously dismayed by DeLaughter's one great error in the Beckwith case— hiding the gun.

The Restroom Scene

Other scenes were entirely made up or expanded from real-life moments. During the actual trial, Bobby DeLaughter and Byron De La Beckwith briefly ran into each other in a courthouse restroom. According to DeLaughter's account, they exchanged only a few tense words.

> "Well, is this jury shaping up to suit you?" Beckwith asked.
>
> "We'll just have to wait and see," DeLaughter said.
>
> "That we will, my boy," Beckwith replied gleefully. "Oh, yes, sir, that we will."[11]

DeLaughter then left the restroom.

In the movie, this scene is considerably lengthened, with Beckwith openly taunting DeLaughter. At one point, DeLaughter reminds Beckwith that it was not a deer he killed in 1963.

Beckwith makes a sinister reply, almost admitting to the murder: "A deer, Mr. DeLaughter, is a beautiful animal—one of God's creatures. I would never kill a deer. A nigger, on the other hand, is another matter entirely." (In fact, Beckwith was an avid hunter.)

Beckwith ends the scene with a sarcastic (and slightly misquoted) echo of Martin Luther King's celebrated "I Have a Dream" speech: "Free at last, free at last; Great God Almighty, I'm free at last!"

Although the scene is almost entirely fictional, it does accurately portray Beckwith's arrogance and the depths of his bigotry. And since Beckwith never testified at the 1994 trial, the expanded restroom encounter gave him a final dramatic moment.

Critical and Public Reaction

"For years I wanted to make a film that dealt with race relations," Reiner said in an interview. "But I didn't feel I had the right to tell the stories of people like Martin Luther King Jr., Malcolm X, or even Medgar Evers, for that matter. But I felt I had the right to tell the story of a white person facing these issues and what he learns about himself. Bobby DeLaughter was my way into this subject matter."[12]

As it happened, this very approach provoked the sharpest criticism of *Ghosts of Mississippi*. Many critics complained that Reiner had simply told the wrong story. The movie, they argued, should have been about Myrlie Evers-Williams and her tireless, decades-long search for justice. It should not have focused on a white male Mississippian's quest for redemption.

As Godfrey Cheshire put it in a review for *Variety*: "When future generations turn to this era's movies for an account of the struggles for racial justice in America, they'll learn the surprising lesson that such battles were fought and won by square-jawed white guys."[13]

Notable Cast Members

In *Ghosts of Mississippi*, Medgar Evers's sons Darrell and James Van Evers played themselves as adults. Yolanda King, daughter of the slain civil rights leader Martin Luther King, Jr., played Evers's daughter Reena as an adult.

Director Rob Reiner with Whoopi Goldberg. Reiner had wanted for years to make a film that dealt with race.

Even the popular and charismatic performer Whoopi Goldberg received unusually harsh criticism. Goldberg described the real-life Myrlie Evers-Williams as having "a huge presence when she enters a room, much like other incredible women such as Shirley Chisholm or Coretta King."[14] But in the movie, wrote critic Roger Ebert: "Myrlie never really emerges except as an emblem, and Goldberg plays her like the guest of honor at a testimonial banquet."[15]

Receiving mixed reviews at best, *Ghosts of Mississippi* was a box-office failure. Nevertheless, Reiner's efforts received favorable comments from someone intimately involved with its story.

"I think Rob Reiner has really done a good job and I sense that he has a lot of integrity for our story," said Medgar Evers's son Darrell. "Justice is a word that can be overused, but I feel that justice has been done. It's a great feeling. And to have a film made about our story is an added boost. It is something we never expected."[16]

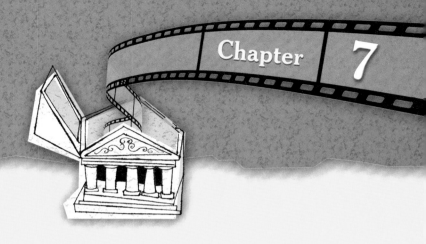

Chapter 7

Too Many Martyrs

Medgar Evers was not a violent man, and he had never encouraged violence in others. That made his murder especially shocking to many people of both races. Publicity about his assassination nudged the South toward change. Myrlie Evers described small, if timid, differences in Mississippi:

> After Medgar's death, almost immediately, things began to change. And as I tell young people that I speak to, it was a significant change, but those things were so minute. For instance, almost immediately, we had school crossing guards. Can you envision a group of people protesting, trying

to get school crossing guards? I mean, that we take for granted today? . . . Shortly thereafter, a few policemen were hired who happen to have been black, but they were restricted to their own neighborhoods.[1]

For African Americans, anger replaced fear of retaliation. Black demonstrators marched to protest Evers's death, and many began to take more active roles in the civil rights movement. Of course, that movement had a long way to go. There would be more violence, but there would also be a federal civil rights bill. Things would change.

The murder of Medgar Evers was especially shocking to many people of both races. Publicity about his assassination nudged the South toward change.

Words and Music

Well-known author Eudora Welty was a native of Jackson, Mississippi. Among other awards, she received a Pulitzer Prize in 1973. Welty died in Jackson in 2001, at age ninety-two.

In 1963, when Eudora Welty heard that Medgar Evers had been murdered, she sat down and started writing. Her story "Where Is the Voice Coming From?" is told from the imagined killer's point of view:

As soon as I heard wheels I knowed who was coming. That was him and bound to be him. It was the right nigger heading in a new white car up his driveway towards his garage with the light shining, but stopping before he got there, maybe not to wake 'em. That was him. I knowed it when

> he put out the car lights and put his foot out and
> I knowed him standing dark against the light. I
> knowed him then like I know me now. I knowed
> him even by his still, listening back. . . .
>
> He had to be the one. He stood right still and
> waited against the light, his back was fixed, fixed
> on me like a preacher's eyeballs when he's yelling,
> "Are you saved?" He's the one.
>
> I'd already brought up my rifle, I'd already
> taken my sights. And I'd already got him. . . .[2]

After shooting his target, Welty's gunman walked over to the dead man and said, "We ain't never now, never going to be equals and you know why? One of us is dead."[3]

Welty's title "Where Is the Voice Coming From?" asked where such hatred comes from. After the murder of Medgar Evers, that question was on many minds. Musicians in New York's Greenwich Village joined the civil rights cause. They played, sang, and recorded their protests.

Folk singers Bob Dylan and Joan Baez both performed at the August 28, 1963, March on Washington for Jobs and Freedom. (One of the organizers of the march, Martin Luther King, Jr., gave his "I Have a Dream" speech from the steps of the Lincoln Memorial on the same day.) Dylan sang "Only a Pawn in Their Game," putting the blame for the murder on Southern politicians:

> The South politician preaches to the poor white man,
> "You got more than the blacks, don't complain.
> You're better than them, you been born with white
>   skin," they explain.
> And the Negro's name
> Is used, it is plain,
> For the politician's gain . . .[4]

Like Eudora Welty, Dylan thought that Medgar Evers's killer must have been a lower-class white man. However, Beckwith's family was not so very different from Welty's. In *Of Long Memory*, reporter Adam Nossiter points out: "It was not necessary to harness the anger of the redneck Mississippian to kill Evers; the genteel classes had plenty of motivation."[5]

Phil Ochs, also from the Greenwich Village folk-music scene, described himself as a "singing journalist." At the July 1963 Newport Folk Festival he sang "Too Many Martyrs" (cowritten with Bob Gibson). His verses about Medgar Evers's life are followed by the chorus:

> Too many martyrs and too many dead,
> Too many lies, too many empty words were said,
> Too many times for too many angry men,
> Oh, let it never be again.[6]

Commemorations

Although some people had tried hard to ignore Medgar Evers, the murdered man would not be forgotten. In 2002, Adam Nossiter wrote:

> Evers's reputation as a person of genuine substance and courage has not diminished over the years. There was not a single blemish to detract from this image. If anything, his stature has grown with the painful realization that, had he lived, he could have made a great contribution to the well-being of his fellow citizens. . . .[7]

In 1970, Medgar Evers College (MEC) was established in Brooklyn, as part of the City University of New York. Although it is open to all ethnic groups, MEC focuses on promoting educational opportunities for African Americans.

Soundtrack: "The Ballad of Medgar Evers"

The *Ghosts of Mississippi* movie soundtrack includes "The Ballad of Medgar Evers" performed by Matthew Jones with the SNCC Freedom Singers. SNCC (Student Nonviolent Coordinating Committee, pronounced "snick") organized sit-ins and other activities during the civil rights movement.

Matthew Jones got involved with the civil rights movement while he was a student at Tennessee State University. He began writing freedom songs in 1961, and in 1963, he organized the Freedom Singers in Atlanta, Georgia. He wrote "The Ballad of Medgar Evers" soon after the murder.

In 1983, a ninety-minute television drama, *For Us the Living: The Story of Medgar Evers*, starred Howard E. Rollins, Jr. The movie was adapted from Myrlie Evers-Williams 1967 book of the same name.

In Jackson, Mississippi, the library in Medgar Evers's former neighborhood was renamed for him. So was the street where the library was located. Local citizens raised money for a life-sized bronze statue of Evers. In June 1992, when the statue was placed in front of the library, a Jackson TV station broadcast a documentary tribute to Medgar Evers. The movie *Ghosts of Mississippi* was released in 1996.

Myrlie Evers-Williams, photographed at *Glamour* magazine's Women of the Year Awards in 2004, has inspired many with her tenacity and strength.

In 2003, the U.S. Senate declared June 9–16 the Medgar Evers National Week of Remembrance. A service at Arlington National Cemetery commemorated the fortieth anniversary of Evers's burial. At Arlington, Myrlie Evers said, "This afternoon is a time of celebration. I hope that you will feel a kind of ecstasy in your heart that we have reached this point in American society."[8]

Jerry Mitchell and Cold Cases

"The Medgar Evers case was a wedge in the dam," said Morris Dees, cofounder of the Southern Poverty Law Center in Montgomery, Alabama. "It gave everyone a tremendous amount of hope."[9] If Byron De La Beckwith could finally be brought to justice, why not others?

Jerry Mitchell kept writing about racially motivated murders from the civil rights era. He won more than twenty national awards for his work and became a sought-after speaker. Mitchell and his investigations have been featured in major newspapers, magazines, and television stories.

In a 2002 PBS interview, Mitchell said he followed up on the cold cases because, he said, "It sticks in my craw for people to kind of get away with crime. And particularly get away with murder."

Mitchell's articles helped arouse interest and gather information on other civil rights cases:

- *1963, Birmingham, Alabama.* A bomb destroyed the Sixteenth Street Baptist Church, killing fourteen-year-olds Addie Mae Collins, Carole Robertson, and Cynthia Wesley, and eleven-year-old Denise McNair. Twelve years later, Alabama attorney general Bill Baxley successfully prosecuted Klan leader Robert

Chambliss for murder. In 2001, Thomas Blanton was also convicted for the crime.

A third suspect, Mark Cherry, claimed that he had been home watching wrestling on television; an alibi witness backed him up. After interviewing Cherry, Jerry Mitchell discovered that no wrestling had been broadcast that night. Cherry was finally convicted of the bombing in 2002.

- *1964, Neshoba County, Mississippi.* Three civil rights workers were beaten, shot, and buried. The three—Andrew Goodman and Michael Schwerner (both white and Jewish) and James Chaney (African American)—had been arrested for supposedly driving over the speed limit. When they were released, Klansmen were waiting for them.

  By the end of 1998, Mitchell had obtained a leaked transcript of the Sam Bowers trial (see Vernon Dahmer case below). In it, he found evidence against Edgar Ray "Preacher" Killen for organizing the 1964 murder. An Illinois high school teacher and three students worked with Mitchell to bring Killen to trial. In 2005, on the forty-first anniversary of the crime, Killen was found guilty of three counts of manslaughter.

- *1964, Meadville, Mississippi.* African-American teenagers Charles Eddie Moore and Henry Hezekiah Dee were hitchhiking when they were forcibly picked up by Klan members. The two nineteen-year-olds were beaten, then chained to a heavy car engine and thrown into a river, still alive. Their bodies were found during the search for Goodman, Schwerner, and Chaney.

  The FBI arrested Klansmen James Ford Seale and Charles Marcus Edwards and turned them over to local authorities. The charges were promptly dismissed and the suspects set free. But neither Jerry Mitchell nor Thomas Moore (Charles Moore's brother) would give up investigating the case.

In 2007, Charles Marcus Edwards confessed to participating in the kidnapping and beating. He named Seale as the one who had weighted the teenagers and thrown them into the river. James Ford Seale was arrested, charged, and convicted of kidnapping and conspiracy. He was sentenced to serve three life terms in prison. Edwards was granted immunity for his testimony.

- *1966, Hattiesburg, Mississippi.* Vernon Dahmer, a successful African-American businessman and NAACP president, died when Klansmen firebombed his house. Dahmer had started a voter registration drive and helped pay poll taxes for those who could not afford them. Although some Klansmen were convicted for the crime, several trials of Imperial Wizard Sam Bowers ended with hung juries. Material in the Mississippi Sovereignty Commission files uncovered by Mitchell helped convict Bowers in 1998.

On January 24, 2007, *Mother Jones* magazine reported: "Mitchell's work has inspired others—journalists, citizens groups, federal and state investigators—to reexamine Klan killings throughout the South. The scorecard so far: 28 arrests leading to 22 convictions."[10]

Charles Evers

In 1969, Medgar Evers's older brother Charles became the first black man elected mayor of a town in Mississippi. Charles Evers commented, "Medgar and I

What Is a Poll Tax?

In general, a poll tax is any fixed-amount tax charged by a government to every adult. Many Southern states charged a poll tax to vote in public elections. In 1964, the Twenty-fourth Amendment to the Constitution outlawed a poll tax for federal elections. U.S. Supreme Court decisions soon extended this ban to state elections.

said many years ago, if we ever end the violent racism in this state, it'll be the greatest state in the world to live. And now, Medgar, I know you're gone, but I'm telling you, son, it's come to pass."[11]

About six years after the 1994 trial, Bobby DeLaughter and Charles Evers traveled together to give a talk for high school students. Charles Evers told DeLaughter that Medgar would be happy to see how black and white people could get along together now. He said Medgar would be happy that Mississippi had a better image. When Bobby DeLaughter asked what Medgar would be sad about, Charles replied:

> To the extent that blacks don't take advantage of the opportunities he died trying to open up for them, like voting, staying in school, and getting an education. He'd be sad at the way they're killing each other.
>
> Do you realize that more young black men have been killed by other young blacks than the Klan ever hoped to kill? If young blacks really want to honor my brother's memory, they will stay in school, stay off drugs, vote, and make something of themselves."[12]

Continuing Violence

White supremacists are still active in most countries where there is a sizable white population. Not all white supremacists agree about what they stand for. Members usually define themselves as being of white European ancestry and claim a natural superiority to people from other cultures or races.

Some white supremacists do not advocate violence. Others will use any means possible to make a point or to support a cause. Although they do not necessarily work together, there are many connections among white-supremacist groups and individuals.

For example, Byron De La Beckwith wrote articles for *Attack!*, a magazine published by the National Alliance. That group is founded on the ideas of Dr. William Pierce's antigovernment book, *The Turner Diaries.* Clippings from Pierce's book were found in Timothy McVeigh's truck after the 1995 Oklahoma City bombing that killed 168 people and injured hundreds. Some phrases from the *Diaries* were highlighted, including, "We can still find them and kill them."[13]

The Legacy of Medgar Evers

Evers was the first of a number of civil rights leaders to be assassinated in the 1960s. Songs, stories, movies, and commemorations kept his story alive, confronting the public with the necessity for improvements in racial relationships.

As the South slowly changed, a wider range of educational opportunities and jobs opened to African Americans. The prosecution of Beckwith led to the

No Jury Will Convict?

In the movie *Ghosts of Mississippi*, Bobby DeLaughter watches a tape of a Medgar Evers speech. Evers mentions the 1955 murder of fourteen-year-old Emmett Till, a case that Evers had investigated. J. W. Milam and Roy Bryant were accused of the crime, but were acquitted in sixty-seven minutes by a jury made up of white men. Soon afterward, Milam and Bryant admitted their guilt in a 1956 *Look Magazine* article for which they were paid four thousand dollars. They could not be retried because of constitutional protections from double jeopardy.

In his speech, Evers says, "White juries have yet to convict a white man in Mississippi guilty of a crime against a Negro." Later in the movie, Beckwith confronts DeLaughter in the men's room of the courthouse. In fictional though typical Beckwith fashion, he sneers, "You ain't never ever gonna get 12 people to convict me of killing a nigger in the state of Mississippi."

But times had changed. Although some racially motivated assassins were never brought to justice, the murderer of Medgar Evers was.

Medgar Evers's family at his grave in Arlington National Cemetery (from left, Reena, Myrlie, James, and Darrell). Evers had arrived home after World War II determined to take a stand against racism.

prosecution of other racially motivated crimes. Changes in the South made the punishment of those criminals possible.

Evers's legacy is especially visible in the state he most loved. Mississippi once had more lynchings than any other place in America. Forty years after Evers's death, that state had the most elected black officials.[14]

The Obsession of Bobby DeLaughter

In 2006, Bobby DeLaughter was the first recipient of the University of Mississippi Law Alumni Public Service Award. In a lecture at the law school, he described how he had investigated the murder of Medgar Evers. DeLaughter also explained why he had become so obsessed with convicting the murderer:

> After talking with Myrlie (Evers) and hearing her recount the tragic events of that night, it was driven home to me that there are some things that not only span races, that not only span people, but span time, as well.[15]

CHAPTER NOTES

1   The Surprise Witness

1. "Mississippi Justice," The University of Mississippi *Law Center News*, Fall, 1999, <http://www.olemiss.edu/depts/law_misc/feturMsA.htm> (June 2, 2007).
2. Bobby DeLaughter, *Never Too Late: A Prosecutor's Story of Justice in the Medgar Evers Case* (New York: Scribner, 2001), p. 267.
3. Ibid.
4. Ibid.
5. Ibid.
6. Emily Yellin, "A Changing South Revisits Its Unsolved Racial Killings," *The New York Times*, November 8, 1999, <http://query.nytimes.com/gst/fullpage.html?res=9F04E7D8153AF93BA35752C1A96F958260> (February 26, 2008).

2   Assassination

1. Bobby DeLaughter, *Never Too Late: A Prosecutor's Story of Justice in the Medgar Evers Case* (New York: Scribner, 2001), p. 281.
2. Ibid., p. 46.
3. Joan Goldsworthy, "Black History: Myrlie Evers-Williams," *Contemporary Black Biography*, Vol. 8, n.d., <http://gale.cengage.com/free_resources/bhm/bio/everswilliams_m.htm> (February 15, 2008).
4. Adam Nossiter, *Of Long Memory: Mississippi and the Murder of Medgar Evers* (Cambridge, Mass.: DaCapo Press, 2002), p. 39.
5. Ibid., p. 44.

6. Ibid., p. 55.
7. Ibid., p. 48.
8. Ibid., p. 60.
9. Ibid., p. 48.
10. Claude Sitton, "Whites Alarmed: Victim Is Shot from Ambush—158 Negro Marchers Seized," *The New York Times*, June 13, 1963.
11. "Beckwith Is Indicted in Slaying of Evers," The Associated Press, *The New York Times*, July 3, 1963, p. 1.

3 Hung Juries

1. "CNN Perspectives: President Kennedy's Civil Rights Speech," June 11, 1963, *CNN.com*, <http://www.cnn.com/SPECIALS/cold.war/episodes/13/documents/jfk.civil/> (June 2, 2007).
2. Adam Nossiter, *Of Long Memory: Mississippi and the Murder of Medgar Evers* (Cambridge, Mass.: DaCapo Press, 2002), p. 111.
3. "With an Even Hand: Brown v. Board at Fifty—Black Monday, 1954," Library of Congress, 2004, <http://www.loc.gov/exhibits/brown/brown-aftermath.html> (March 6, 2008).
4. Nossiter, p. 91.
5. Ibid., p. 92.
6. Ibid., p. 119.
7. Bobby DeLaughter, *Never Too Late: A Prosecutor's Story of Justice in the Medgar Evers Case* (New York: Scribner, 2001), p. 41.
8. Joan Goldsworthy, "Black History: Myrlie Evers-Williams," *Contemporary Black Biography*, Vol. 8, n.d., <http://gale.cengage.com/free_resources/bhm/bio/everswilliams_m.htm> (February 15, 2008).
9. DeLaughter, p. 19.
10. Jerry Mitchell to interviewer Terrence Smith, Online Focus, April 18, 2002, *A NewsHour with Jim Lehrer* Transcript, <http://www.pbs.org/newshour/media/clarion/mitchell.html> (June 2, 2007).
11. DeLaughter, p. 29.
12. Ibid., p. 27.

13. Ibid., p. 28.

 His Own Words

1. Adam Nossiter, *Of Long Memory: Mississippi and the Murder of Medgar Evers* (Cambridge, Mass.: DaCapo Press, 2002), p. 199.
2. Bobby DeLaughter, *Never Too Late: A Prosecutor's Story of Justice in the Medgar Evers Case* (New York: Scribner, 2001), p. 23.
3. Ibid., p. 60.
4. Ibid., p. 83.
5. Nossiter, p. 243.
6. DeLaughter, p. 195.
7. Elaine Davenport, "The Six New Witnesses," *Southern Changes*, Vol. 16, No. 1, 1994, pp. 10–11, <http://beck.library. emory.edu/southernchanges/article.php?id=sc16-1_004&mdid=sc16-1_001> (June 2, 2007).
8. Ibid.
9. Ibid.
10. Ronald Smothers, "Witnesses Recall Boasts on '63 Killing," *The New York Times*, February 2, 1994, <http://query.ny times.com/gst/fullpage.html?res=9C0DE0DE1339F931A3575 1C0A962958260&scp=1&sq=Smothers+%22Witnesses+Re call+Boasts%22&st=nyt> (March 8, 2008).
11. Davenport, "The Six New Witnesses."
12. Ronald Smothers, "'63 Murder Case Goes to the Jury," *The New York Times*, February 5, 1994, <http://query.nytimes. com/gst/fullpage.html?res=9505EEDC1E39F936A35751 C0A962958260&scp=1&sq=Smothers%2C+%93%9163+ Murder+Case+Goes+To+The+Jury%2C%94&st=nyt> (March 8, 2008).
13. Ronald Smothers, "'63 Murder Case Goes to the Jury."
14. DeLaughter, p. 285.

 Is It Ever Too Late?

1. Ronald Smothers, "'63 Murder Case Goes to the Jury," *The New York Times*, February 5, 1994.

2. Bobby DeLaughter, *Never Too Late: A Prosecutor's Story of Justice in the Medgar Evers Case* (New York: Scribner, 2001), p. 285.
3. Ibid., p. 287.
4. Ibid., p. 288.
5. Ibid.
6. Ibid., p. 207.
7. Ibid., p. 293.
8. Ibid., pp. 293–294.
9. Ibid., p.185.
10. "Myrlie Evers-Williams," NAACP, n.d., <http://www.naacp.org/about/history/mew/> (March 7, 2008).
11. Adam Nossiter, *Of Long Memory: Mississippi and the Murder of Medgar Evers* (Cambridge, Mass.: DaCapo Press, 2002), p. 11.
12. Ibid., p. 12.
13. Byron De La Beckwith, letter to his son, June 15, 1999, <http://www.nationalist.org/docs/history/beckwith.html#Right> (June 3, 2007).
14. Nossiter, p. 259.
15. DeLaughter, p. 291.
16. Ibid., p. 292.
17. Ibid., p. 297.

 ## Ghosts of Mississippi

1. "Willie Morris," *The Mississippi Writers Page*, August 2001, <http://www.olemiss.edu/depts/english/ms-writers/dir/morris_willie/> (July 12, 2008).
2. Rick Bragg, "To Bind Up a Nation's Wound With Celluloid," *The New York Times*, June 16, 1996, <http://select.nytimes.com/search/restricted/article?res=F50E13FE3F5D0C758DDDAF0894DE494D81> (July 2, 2007), and IMBd, trivia for *Ghosts of Mississippi*, <http://www.imdb.com/title/tt0116410/trivia> (June 2, 2007).
3. Bragg.
4. Ibid.

5. "Righting a Wrong: Ghosts of Mississippi," *about . . . time Magazine*, December 1996/January 1997, <http://www.abouttimemag.com/decart.html> (June 2, 2007).

6. Graham Fuller, "Ghosts of Past and Present: Interviews With Whoopi Goldberg and Rob Reiner," *Interview*, January 1997, <http://findarticles.com/p/articles/mi_m1285/is_n1_v27/ai_19121817> (July 2, 2007).

7. Ibid.

8. Bragg.

9. "Righting a Wrong: Ghosts of Mississippi."

10. Bobby DeLaughter, *Never Too Late: A Prosecutor's Story of Justice in the Medgar Evers Case* (New York: Scribner, 2001), p. 88.

11. Ibid., p. 231.

12. "Righting a Wrong: Ghosts of Mississippi."

13. Godfrey Cheshire, "*Ghosts of Mississippi*," *Variety*, December 22, 1996, <http://www.variety.com/review/VE1117436727.html?categoryid=31&cs=1&p=0> (June 3, 2007).

14. "Righting a Wrong: Ghosts of Mississippi."

15. Roger Ebert, "*Ghosts of Mississippi*," *rogerebert.com*, December 20, 1996, <http://rogerebert.suntimes.com/apps/pbcs.dll/article?AID=/19961220/REVIEWS/612200303/1023> (June 3, 2007).

16. "Righting a Wrong: Ghosts of Mississippi."

 Too Many Martyrs

1. Myrlie Evers-Williams on *The News Hour*, PBS, April 23, 2002, <http://www.pbs.org/newshour/media/clarion/myrlie_evers.html> (July 3, 2007).

2. Eudora Welty, "Where Is the Voice Coming From?" *The Collected Stories of Eudora Welty* (New York: Harcourt Brace Jovanovich, 1980), p. 604.

3. Ibid.

4. Bob Dylan, "Only a Pawn in Their Game," lyrics as performed by Bob Dylan during the March on Washington, Lincoln Memorial, Washington, D.C., August 28, 1963; transcribed by Manfred Helfert, <http://www.bobdylanroots.com/pawn.html> (June 3, 2007).

5. Adam Nossiter, *Of Long Memory: Mississippi and the Murder of Medgar Evers* (Cambridge, Mass.: DaCapo Press, 2002), p. 108.

6. Phil Ochs, "Too Many Martyrs," Lyrics transcribed by Manfred Helfert from version performed by at Newport Folk Festival, July 26–28, 1963, <http://www.fortunecity.com/tinpan/parton/2/evers.html> (June 3, 2007).

7. Nossiter, p. 260.

8. Myrlie Evers in "Medgar Evers Remembered in Ceremony at Gravesite," *The New York Times*, June 17, 2003.

9. Emily Yellin, "A Changing South Revisits Its Unsolved Racial Killings," *The New York Times*, November 8, 1999, <http://www.rickrowww.nationalist.org ss.com/reference/kkk/kkk16.html> (June 3, 2007).

10. Joe Treen, "Southern Man: Klan-Busting Journalist Jerry Mitchell," *Mother Jones*, January 24, 2007, <http://www.motherjones.com/news/update/2007/01/jerry_mitchell.html> (June 3, 2007).

11. "The Legacy of Medgar Evers: 40 Years After Civil Rights Leader's Death, a Changed Mississippi," *All Things Considered*, NPR, June 10, 2003, <http://www.npr.org/templates/story/story.php?storyId=1294360> (May 5, 2008).

12. Bobby DeLaughter, *Never Too Late: A Prosecutor's Story of Justice in the Medgar Evers Case* (New York: Scribner, 2001), pp. 294–295.

13. "'Turner Diaries' introduced in McVeigh trial," CNN, April 28, 1997, <http://www.cnn.com/US/9704/28/okc/> (June 3, 2007).

14. "The Legacy of Medgar Evers: 40 Years After Civil Rights Leader's Death, a Changed Mississippi."

15. "Mississippi Justice," The University of Mississippi, *Law Center News*, Fall, 1999, <http://www.olemiss.edu/depts/law_misc/feturMsA.htm> (June 2, 2007).

GLOSSARY

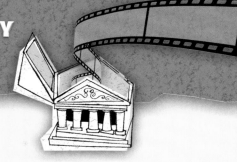

acquit—To find not guilty; free of criminal charges.

appeal—To apply to a higher court for a reversal of the decision of a lower court.

appeals court—A court that hears appeals of decisions from a lower court.

arraignment—The defendant's first appearance before a judge to be informed of the charges. The question of bail and any request for court-appointed attorneys are decided at the arraignment.

authenticated—Testimony showing a judge that an item of evidence is genuine and has a valid connection to the case.

autopsy—A postmortem examination to discover the cause of death or the extent of disease.

bail—Money paid to a court as security that a released defendant will appear at all future hearings.

custody—Legal guardianship of a child (custody also can mean imprisonment).

defendant—The person or group accused of a crime in a court of law.

defense—Information presented in court to deny the charges against the accused; the attorneys or others arguing for the defendant (the person accused of a crime).

district attorney—A local public official who prosecutes cases for the government.

evidence—Information or objects used to prove or disprove facts in a case.

extradition—The process of handing over a person from one state (or nation) to authorities in another state (or nation) where that person has been accused or convicted of a crime.

federalize—Put under federal (national government) control.

grand jury—A group of citizens selected to consider a prosecutor's evidence and decide whether the evidence is sufficient for the case to be taken to trial.

indict—To formally charge with a felony (a serious crime that is severely punished).

integration—Opening a group or location to all regardless of race, ethnicity, religion, gender, or social class.

jury tampering—Attempting to illegally manipulate the makeup of a jury or the decisions of a juror.

lynching—A mob killing of a person for an offense they believe has been committed, with or without a legal trial. Lynching is often carried out by hanging.

prosecution—Legal proceeding against a person accused of a criminal offense; the lawyers who argue the case against the accused.

reasonable doubt—Doubt based upon reasoning and common sense after considering the evidence in a case. To vote "guilty," a juror must be certain beyond a reasonable doubt of the defendant's guilt.

segregation—The practice of keeping races apart, especially through separate housing and separate public facilities such as schools and transportation.

sentence—Punishment ordered by a court for a defendant who has been convicted of a crime.

summation—An attorney's closing speech at the conclusion of a trial.

testify—To make a statement of fact based on personal experience that can be used as evidence in a court of law.

verdict—The decision of the jury on the case being tried.

witness—A person who has seen or heard an event take place; one who testifies under oath in a court of law.

FURTHER READING

Books

Finlayson, Reggie. *We Shall Overcome: The History of the American Civil Rights Movement* (Minneapolis: Lerner Publications), 2003.

Moore, Heidi. *Medgar Evers* (Chicago: Heinemann Library), 2006.

Nelson, Marilyn. *A Wreath for Emmett Till* (Boston: Houghton Mifflin), 2005.

Ribeiro, Myra. *The Assassination of Medgar Evers* (New York: Rosen Publishing Group), 2002.

Internet Addresses

Ghosts of Mississippi
<http://www.imdb.com/title/tt0116410>

The Mississippi Writers Page: Medgar Evers
<http://www.olemiss.edu/depts/english/ms-writers/dir/evers_medgar/>

National Association for the Advancement of Colored People
<http://www.naacp.org>